CAN THE SILENCE OF AN ACCUSED SPUR THE DECISION OF GUILT IN ENGLAND, BELGIUM, AND THE UNITED STATES?

BÉNÉDICTE MBANGALA

CAN THE SILENCE OF AN ACCUSED SPUR THE DECISION OF GUILT IN ENGLAND, BELGIUM, AND THE UNITED STATES? [1]

ISBN: 978-1-948915-25-0

NORTH
AMERICAN BUSINESS
PRESS

North American Business Press
Atlanta, Georgia
Miami, Florida
New York New York,
Toronto, Canada

FIRST PRINTING, 2022

Dedication

To my mom and dad, being your daughter is my greatest joy.
Thank you for always seeing what I can't see in myself.

To my sister and my brothers, you have been my greatest force during the darkest days.
I love you the most.

Abstract

What do we think of the assertion that a man who remains silent is necessarily prompted by a desire to conceal a truth, or even to stifle his potential guilt, which only a maintained silence could succeed in covering up? What about the attitude of drawing negative conclusions from a refusal to speak and interpreting the silence of an accused person as an admission of guilt? Known as the "Droit au silence" in Belgium, the "Right of Silence" in England, and the "Fifth" in the United States, this right is considered to be one of the fundamental procedural guarantees in criminal proceedings. From then on, the question has arisen as to whether in England, Belgium and the United States, the exercise of the right to silence can be interpreted to the detriment of the accused, to the point of spurring a decision of guilt against such an accused person. This dissertation offers to answer this problem statement in four chapters. (i) The right to silence as one of the bulwarks of the criminal defense (ii) The right to silence, strongly affirmed in Strasbourg case law (iii) Consecration of the right to silence in England, the United States and Belgium (iv) Cross-sectional analysis. Two recent criminal cases shall also be discussed (the attack on the Jewish Museum: Medhi Nemmouche and the indictment of Donald Trump's lawyer, Michael Cohen, in the "stormygate" case) in order to compare our teachings with facts that have recently marked the news...

Table of Contents

Introduction

What do we think of the assertion that a man who remains silent is necessarily prompted by a desire to conceal a truth, or even to stifle his potential guilt, which only a maintained silence could succeed in covering up? What about the attitude of drawing negative conclusions from a refusal to speak and interpreting the silence of an accused person as an admission of guilt?

This would imply that there is much more to silence than the act of deciding not to speak. There would be, for the one who opts for this silence, underlines *Dinouart*, "a certain know-how; that of controlling his tongue, taking the moments which are convenient to retain it or to give it a moderate freedom; of following the rules which prudence prescribes in this matter; of distinguishing, in the events of life, the situations wherein silence must be inviolable; of having an inflexible firmness, when it comes to observing, without denying oneself, all that one has judged suitable to keep silent"[2].

In law, silence has long been considered to be equivalent to confession[3]. In his 1823 Treaty, Bentham again said that "silence is synonymous with confession. Confession is an oral admission [of crime]; silence a confession of fact"[4]. However, this truth was challenged from the 16th century onwards, particularly following the rejection of the use of torture, which was practiced in Western Europe, when the authorities wanted to obtain the confession of an accused person.

From now on, speaking freely without being coerced is one of the fundamental rights available to human beings[5]. Silence, which is its corollary, should therefore be no less. In this regard, *Carbonnier* maintained that "silence must be conceived as the freedom of inner thought; there is no value that is superior to it"[6]. *Louis Edmont Pettiti*, meanwhile, asserts that silence is the power given to the human being to meditate without uttering a word. If words are at the center of one's personality, he says, its counter-face is indeed silence and correlatively, the possibility of keeping it[7].

Although the perception of silence as a confession has finally been abandoned, there is a form of orality in silence, "a somewhat negative orality"[8]. In this way, "the reception of a person's silence by others can be the source of various interpretations, which are themselves marked by subjectivity"[9]. This reality is all the more prevalent in criminal law, since the fact of remaining silent has become a real faculty, a possibility for the accused to preserve his or her silence in order to be protected from the risks of any statement that could contribute to establishing his or her own incrimination. This is the consecration of the right to silence and the prohibition against self-incrimination in positive law. In the developments that follow, we will see how this right is considered to be one of the major elements of the criminal proceedings[10].

The main question we are concerned with is the accused person's right to silence and the possibility of the prosecuting authorities[11], to draw unfavorable conclusions about him/her. Our question is formulated in the following terms: **can the silence of an accused person be a reason for a decision of guilt in England, Belgium, and the United States?** In other words, in these three countries, can the exercise of the right to silence be interpreted as a sign of guilt on the part of the person exercising it?

This dissertation proposes to answer this question in four chapters. The first chapter is intended to provide a definition of the right to silence as well as clarifications on its relationship with the principle of the presumption of innocence and the rights of the defense. The second chapter discusses the major lessons of the right to silence from the case law of the European Court of Human Rights. The third chapter focuses on the study of the right to silence in Belgian, British, and American criminal law. Finally, the fourth and last chapter provides a transversal analysis of the issue of the right to silence in the three above-mentioned countries. It also mentions two real cases in order to allow us to compare our teachings with concrete cases that have been in the news.

Let the reader take note in advance that the question of the right to silence and the privilege against self-incrimination studied in the light of Belgian, British, or American law is a vast topic. Therefore, it will not be possible to elucidate all of its mysteries. Therefore, this dissertation does not focus on a philosophical or psychological study of the issue, but rather on its legal aspect - insofar as it is possible to detach this aspect from the preceding ones. Moreover, it should be specified that the developments that will build this dissertation, without claiming to be exhaustive despite the contribution of past and present doctrinal contributions, will modestly attempt to draw the legal consequences of the exercise of silence, thus bringing up the elements of reflection to the previously asked question, being the main subject of this study.

Before beginning our study, a few terminological clarifications must be made.

- **The right to silence and the right not to contribute to one's own incrimination** are generally invoked together. Although they are closely related, it is important to distinguish them. The right to remain silent is one aspect of the right not to contribute towards one's own incrimination, which is much broader than the simple right to remain silent[12]. Indeed, it includes the right to remain silent as well as the right not to produce documents against oneself[13]. It will be referred to more as the "right to silence" or the "right to remain silent". Nevertheless, there is no doubt that these terms will echo the right not to contribute to one's own incrimination that follows.
- The term "**accused**" used in this paper refers to an individual who is the subject of criminal proceedings, although the legal orders and jurisdictions examined use different terms to refer to such a person.

1. The right to silence as one of the bulwarks of the criminal defense

1.1 Definition of the right to silence

Attempting to define the right to silence would presuppose a common and shared acceptance of the very notion of the word silence. However, silence covers multiple realities. "There is the silence before any word, the silence in thoughts, the silence that supports listening and makes the other's word to exist, the silence of the unspoken, the silence of disapproval, the silence of complicity, the silence of embarrassment, of shyness, of indifference, the imposed silence, the silence of those who are voiceless, the heavy silence of family secrets, the silence of the tortured resistance fighter who refuses to give the name of his accomplices..."[14]. In the context of this dissertation, we note that silence is "the state of a person who refrains from corresponding. Figuratively speaking, the cessation of all noise"[15]. Let us now leave the sphere of common sense to see what the right to silence is in Belgian criminal law.

1.1.1 Legal basis of the right to silence

As we have seen above, reflecting on the very notion of silence reveals the complexity of the concept. This justifies the difficulty, in Belgian law, of defining the very notion of a right to silence[16].

As far as the definition is concerned, it is considered that the right to silence is the recognition of a right, for a person, not to be required to provide information, nor to answer questions or make spontaneous statements that could be used to establish the existence of facts against him or her, which could lead to a criminal sanction, or simply to consolidate proceedings against him or her[17]. Moreover, the right to silence *sensu lato* can also take the form of a refusal to express oneself in writing.[18]

For the sake of completeness, it should be added that the right to silence is also the right of the defendant to organize his defense as he sees fit, without incurring sanctions or prosecution if he chooses to adopt an entirely passive attitude during the various interrogations addressed to him[19].

As for its legal basis, the right to silence is found in international law, in this case in article 14, 3, g, of the International Covenant on Civil and Political Rights, which spells it out[20].

Adopted by the United Nations General Assembly, this pact "is intended to apply throughout the world and its provisions are directly applicable in domestic law"[21]. This is especially true for Belgium, which ratified the pact on April 21, 1983. The rulings handed down by the Constitutional Court and the Court of Cassation show that reference is regularly made to this Convention[22].

Curious as it may seem, there is no mention of the right to silence in the European Convention on Human Rights. This right is "silent"[23]. In Belgian law, Article 47bis of the Code of Criminal Procedure, inserted by the law of March 12, 1998, mentions this right[24].

1.1.2 Scope of application

The application scope of the right to silence must be defined not only materially (1.1.2.1.), but also ratione personae (1.1.2.2.).

1.1.2.1 Ratione materiae

In terms of *ratione materiae*, certain states "of Romano-Germanic obedience, limit the application scope of the right to silence to criminal matters, while others, attached to the Anglo-Saxon legal tradition, extend it to different fields"[25]. In Belgian law, we note that the right to silence is exercised with a predilection for criminal law, a field in which it is recognized in the law of democratic states[26].

As for the European Court of Human Rights, through its singular conception of criminal law, it tends to broaden its scope of application[27]. The Court imposes respect for the right to silence, while admitting that this right cannot be applied to certain non-criminal proceedings (purely administrative or disciplinary proceedings, for example) [28]. This is on the condition, however, that evidence gathered in violation of the right to silence during such proceedings is not subsequently used in criminal proceedings [29].

Finally, this same Court does not fail to add that all offences will be covered by the right to remain silent, which is itself applicable throughout the proceedings (police and judicial phase)[30].

1.1.2.2 Ratione personae

In terms of Ratione personae, the right to silence is not approached in exactly the same way, depending on whether the person claiming it is a witness (1.1.2.2.1.), a suspect (1.1.2.2.2.) or an accused (1.1.2.2.3.).

1.1.2.2.1 The witness's right to silence

The recognition of the witness's right to silence has been the subject of several debates since in this hypothesis, two fundamental values clash[31]. On the one hand, the sense of personal preservation, and on the other, the imperatives of the search for the truth[32].

At present, it is considered that, although he/she is obliged to testify sincerely, the witness can never be forced to reveal facts that are likely to be held against him/her[33]. However, some authors qualify this statement by stating that this right may be difficult to implement when "a beginning of explanation on the reasons for his/her desire to remain silent seems similar to a confession which he/she forbids him-/herself from making"[34].

It is interesting to mention a few cases in Belgian law that mark the reflection of the Court of Cassation on the recognition of a right to silence for the benefit of the witness. Two cases will be considered. The Mortier ruling, handed down in 1881, concerned a witness who was forced, in court, to alter the truth in order not to incriminate himself[35]. The cassation plaintiff had been convicted of perjury by the Ghent Court of Appeal[36]. The Court of Cassation upheld this decision, considering that it was wrong to believe that there is no false testimony when a witness alters the truth in order to avoid incriminating him-/herself [37]. According to the Court of Cassation, "in line with the text as well as the spirit of the law, it is impossible to admit that, under the pretext of not wanting to expose him-/herself to criminal prosecution, a witness can violate with impunity the duties imposed on him by the sanctity of the oath, knowingly alter the truth, deceive the judges and expose them to endanger the fortune or honor, the liberty or the life of the citizens"[38].

Following this case, the Court of Cassation handed down the Desclée decision, wherein it reversed its jurisprudence[39]. This case also concerned a person heard as a witness, this time by an investigating judge. The said witness was accused of having refused to answer a question put to him[40]. According to the Court of Cassation, "respect for the rights of defense and the social need to ensure the sincerity of testimony prohibited the obtention of confessions from witnesses by the use of physical or moral coercion"[41]. This rule was violated in this case, since a person called to testify under oath was necessarily placed in the alternative of either altering the truth by perjuring himself or making revelations of a compromising nature[42]. Finally, the Court held that the duty to answer questions be interrupted if, when questioned about a specific fact, the witness being heard under oath finds him-/herself in a situation where he can only answer with complete truth by exposing himself to prosecution[43]. *Ultimately,* the witness heard under oath has the sole right not to answer a specific incriminating question [44]. However, he does not have the right to systematically refuse to answer the questions put to him[45].

1.1.2.2.2 The suspect's right to silence

The term suspect is understood to mean a person who, in criminal proceedings, is questioned by the police as a person against whom there is a suspicion of guilt[46]. In other words, the person is heard. In other words, the person is heard, but not charged. In Belgian law, as we recall, it is the current article 47 bis of the Code of Criminal Procedures which states in its paragraphs two and three that a suspect, whether deprived of his liberty or not, has the choice, after having declared his identity, to make a statement, to answer the questions put to him or to remain silent, and that he cannot be forced to accuse himself. Before the hearing takes place, these faculties must be communicated to him[47].

In the jurisprudence of the European Court of Human Rights, it is considered that the right to silence and the right against self-incrimination of the suspect do not extend to "pieces of information which exist independently of the suspect's will"[48]. Thus, minimal physical harm may be done for the purposes of the case. It is understood, of course, that inhumane or degrading treatment for the obtention of this information does not fall within the scope of this acceptance of minimal harm[49]. For example, the forceful and brutal administration of an emetic to the suspect in order to make him regurgitate a bag of heroin has been condemned by the European Court of Human Rights, which considered that this treatment was tantamount to a violation of Article 3 of the European Convention on Human Rights[50]. In the same way, abusive coercion resulting from obliging a suspect to speak under the threat of criminal sanction is prohibited[51].

1.1.2.2.3 The accused's right to silence

Belgian jurisprudence recognizes a right to silence for the accused and the defendant. Several rulings illustrate this. Assuming that the accused cannot be compelled to confess guilt, his examination under oath must be rejected, since to do otherwise would have the effect of putting him in the alternative of either perjuring himself or accusing himself[52]. As an example, we can cite the Navez case, in which the Court of Cassation ruled that a defendant cannot be forced to testify against himself under penalty of violation of articles 14 §3, g of the International Covenant on Civil and Political Rights and article 6, §1 of the European Convention on Human Rights[53]. The same applies to the Agusta-Dassault ruling, wherein the Court of Cassation, ruling in combined chambers, declared that "the hearing under oath of a person under judicial investigation violates the general principle of the rights of defense when the oath thus taken compels the person being heard to testify against him-/herself or to admit guilt"[54].

As for the Strasbourg judges, they have consistently admitted that any person accused of an offence may invoke the right to silence[55].

With the definition of the right to silence as well as its various application scopes having been mentioned, we will now look at the link between the right to silence, the presumption of innocence and the rights of defense.

1.2 The link between the right to silence, the presumption of innocence and the rights of defense

1.2.1 Right to silence and presumption of innocence

Article 6 of the European Convention on Human Rights expresses a fundamental rule:

"Anyone charged with an offence shall be presumed innocent until proven guilty by law"[56]. Article 2 of the International Covenant on Civil and Political Rights repeats the same provision[57]. These articles refer to the fundamental principle in criminal law, which is the presumption of innocence. The latter does not mean that one must absolutely believe in the innocence of the accused person, but that, as long as a ruling in good and due form has not legally established the guilt of the individual in question, he or she should be treated as not guilty[58]. Compliance with this principle is required in order to ensure the protection of the rights of the accused. This principle must be respected throughout the proceedings until a final conviction is reached[59]. The preparatory phase of the trial is therefore also covered in the respect of the presumption of innocence[60].

This principle, because of its fundamental character in criminal law, must be adhered to not only by the judicial authorities (including the public prosecutor), but also by the public authorities[61].

It follows from this principle that since the individual is presumed innocent, the burden of proof does not rest on him or her, but rather on the party seeking to rebut this presumption, in other words, the prosecuting party[62]. This rule inevitably strengthens the position of the accused in the face of the prosecution authorities[63]. It even implies that "he/she is not required to prove the reality of the justification or excuse from which he/she intends to benefit. The onus is on the public prosecutor to prove that this allegation is inaccurate"[64]

Now that this principle has been recalled, a link must be made between the presumption of innocence and the right to silence. Indeed, the two are closely linked. Since the accused is not obliged to collaborate in the administration of evidence, he or she may be content to remain silent without worrying about having to prove his or her innocence, thereby adopting a purely passive contestation role[65]. The European Court of Human Rights, in affirming that the right not to incriminate oneself is directly deduced from the presumption of innocence, reaffirms the existence of this close link between the right to silence and the presumption of innocence[66].

As for the passive attitude that the presumed innocent may adopt, a minority opinion sees in this posture granted by the right to silence and the prohibition against self-incrimination, a possibility of going so far as to lie, without this lie being punishable[67]. In this respect, it seems to us coherent that the individual to whom a right to silence and a right against self-incrimination is recognized can alter the truth in order not to self-incriminate. Indeed, what would remain of this right if such an attitude were systematically prohibited?

We conclude this section on the presumption of innocence by affirming that this principle must be regarded, like the principle of criminal legality, as one of the indispensable foundations of criminal law[68]. "Its purpose being both to ensure the safety of individuals against arbitrariness by protecting personal freedoms, and to stimulate the search for the exact judicial truth by avoiding, as far as possible, the risks of error that would easily be generated by the systemic belief in the guilt of the prosecuted individuals"[69].

1.2.2 The right to silence and the right of defense

The right of defense is a general principle of law that consists of "freely supporting or opposing a claim before the judge"[70]. "The imperative of respecting the rights of defense is one of the most solid foundations of the right to silence[71]. Indeed, the right to remain silent can be a safeguard against possible abuses during interrogations[72]. It is for this reason that it appears to be "a prelude to a judicious organization of the defense"[73] and is one of the strategies that can be adopted by a party under these same rights, as considered by the Court of Cassation itself [74]. This can be illustrated by a decision of the Court of Cassation which overturned the decision of the Court of Appeal wherein a person had been penalized "because of the adopted system of defense and, more particularly, because she denied her guilt"[75]. On this occasion, "the Court of Cassation declared the first part of the plea [right of defense] to be well-founded, on the grounds that the contested ruling indirectly challenged the right of the plaintiff, who did not have the burden of proof, to freely express what she considered useful for the exercise of her right of defense and to organize this defense as she saw fit".[76] Through this decision, the Court recognizes the right of the accused/defendant to freely express whatever he considers useful for the exercise of his right of defense and to organize his defense as he sees fit, "even by exercising his right to silence"[77].

The right to silence, the right to the presumption of innocence as well as the right of defense are therefore fundamental rights in criminal law and are closely linked.

However, the right to silence cannot be addressed without mentioning the correlative obligation to notify its beneficiary. Indeed, how can one ensure that the accused can become aware of his right and exercise it if he is not informed of it?

We now turn to the necessity of notifying the right to silence to the accused to ensure its effectiveness.

1.3 A right to be notified to ensure its effectiveness

The notification of the right to silence is a real issue since it allows the beneficiary to become aware of the possession of his right, and by so doing, bringing it to life[78]. This notification is therefore inherent to the right itself[79].

The jurisprudence of the European Court of Human Rights in this regard maintains that there is a link between the notification of the right to silence and the presence of the lawyer: when the lawyer is absent, the absence of this notification is noted[80]. Indeed, remaining silent is one thing, but one still needs to know why and how to do so; in this sense, the lawyer's role is of major importance.

This is all the more valid for the Belgian law, which has hastened to modify its legislation to comply with the requirements of the *Salduz v. Turkey* case of 27 November 2008 by the European Court of Human Rights[81]. This case represents the emblematic decision on the right to legal assistance during initial interrogations. It argues, among other things, that "in most cases, the particular vulnerability in which an accused person finds him-/herself can only be adequately compensated for by the assistance of a lawyer, whose task, among other things, is to ensure that the right of every accused person not to incriminate him-/herself is respected"[82].

As a result of this case law, national legislation is now required, "unless it can be shown, in the light of particular circumstances, that there are compelling reasons for restricting this right"[83], to guarantee the assistance of a lawyer from the very first police interrogation onwards [84].

Although the European Court of Human Rights considers the rights not to contribute to one's own incrimination, the right to remain silent and the right to legal counsel as being independent, it does not fail to note their complementarity. The famous phrase "I will speak only in the presence of a lawyer" therefore makes it possible to understand the link between these rights[85].

Belgium so far had no similar obligation in its legislation [86]. It had to adapt its legislation [87]. This was followed by the adoption of the first "Salduz" law of 13 April 2011, which came into force on 1 January 2012[88]. In the wake of this, a European Union directive of October 22, 2013, also devoted to the right to legal assistance from the earliest stages of criminal proceedings, was adopted [89]. This new directive, given the advance in relation to the requirements prescribed by the European Court of Human Rights that it embodied, led to an amendment of the Belgian text. This amendment resulted in the law of November 21, 2016, on certain rights of persons under interrogation, the so-called "Salduz-bis"[90]. This law provides, among other things, for the assistance of a lawyer for any person being questioned and for all hearings with a criminal purpose if the facts concerned are punishable by a custodial sentence. The role of the lawyer is more pronounced, and he/she is responsible for ensuring that the person questioned does not accuse him-/herself, and that he/she is free to answer the questions put to him/her or to exercise his/her right to remain silent[91].

Thus, the European Court of Human Rights found a violation of Article 6 in a case wherein the plaintiff confessed to stealing fuel while being questioned by the police on the side of the road without being informed of his right to remain silent[92]. Of course, there was no lawyer by his side[93]. The Court found that "in the circumstances of this case, it was incumbent upon the police to inform the applicant of the privilege against self-incrimination and the right to remain silent[94]. In the Brusco ruling, the same Court recalled that "the person in police custody has the right to be assisted by a lawyer from the outset of the action and during questioning, this a fortiori when he/she has not been informed by the authorities of his/her right to remain silent, and stresses that in this case, the confession was obtained in the absence of the lawyer, who was therefore unable to inform his/her client of his/her right to remain silent and not to incriminate him-/herself before his/her first interrogation[95].

The previous pages have enabled us to take interest in the definition of the right to silence and its relationship to the presumption of innocence, and the rights of defense. We observed that this guarantee could hardly be effective if it was not notified to the accused.

It is now a question of studying how the right to silence has been strongly stated in the jurisprudence of the European Court of Human Rights. This proclamation of the right to remain silent within this Court is not without consequences for the States[96].

Indeed, Belgian judges are strongly inspired by the solutions adopted in Strasbourg when they themselves have to rule on the violation of such a right. This is therefore the relevance of studying the case law of the European Court of Human Rights.

2. The right to silence strongly affirmed in Strasbourg case law

Following the developments devoted to the *right to silence as one of the bulwarks of the criminal defense*, we thought it would be useful to continue by looking at the three founding rulings on the right to silence in the case law of the European Court of Human Rights, as well as by analyzing four other rulings in the case law of the same Court.

2.1 The three founding rulings

This section focuses on the Funke (2.1.1.), Murray (2.1.2.) and Saunders (2.1.3.) rulings, given their contribution to the issue of the right to silence and the right not to contribute to one's own incrimination.

2.1.1 Funke ruling[97]

As early as 1992, the European Commission of Human Rights spoke to deduce from article 10 of the European Convention on Human Rights, relating to the right to freedom of expression, a right not to be forced to express oneself[98].

In this case, Mr. Jean-Gustave Funke, a German national, worked as a sales representative and lived in France, in Lingolsheim (Bas-Rhin)[99].

On January 14, 1980, three Strasbourg customs officers accompanied by a judicial police officer went to the home of the applicant and his wife to obtain details of their assets abroad[100]. On this occasion, Mr. Funke admitted having held several bank accounts abroad. He also stated that he did not have any records of these accounts at home, and that he refused to provide records of his various bank accounts held abroad anyway[101]. The customs officers searched the premises and discovered the statements and checkbooks from foreign banks, as well as the invoice for a car repair in Germany and two cameras. The customs officers finally seized these documents and objects and issued an official report on the same day.

On May 3, 1982, the customs administration summoned Mr. Funke before the Strasbourg police court, for the purpose of ordering him to pay a fine of 50 French francs per day until the account statements were produced; it also presented an order for committal to prison[102]. On September 27, 1982, the court imposed a fine of 1,200 francs on the petitioner and ordered him to produce to the customs administration the bank statements of the *Société de Banque Suisse* in Basel, the Deutsche Bank in Warsaw, the savings account at the *Württembergische Bausparkasse in Leonberg* (FRG), as well as any document concerning the financing of his apartment acquired in Schonach (FRG), under penalty of a fine of 20 francs per day of delay[103].

Mr. Funke considered himself to be the victim of a violation of Article 6, §§1 and 2 of the European Convention on Human Rights[104].

With regard to Article 6, paragraph 1, the applicant argued that his right to a fair trial had been violated. According to him, the administration had violated his right not to testify against himself, and thus his right to silence, by forcing him to collaborate in his own prosecution by producing the documents in question. In his view, this manner of acting could not be considered to be in conformity with the requirements of Article 6, especially since the French authorities could have had recourse to international mutual assistance and could themselves have collected the necessary evidence from foreign states[105].

The French government, for its part, insisted on the declarative nature of the customs regime, which entails a series of duties such as the duty of those subject to the regime to keep documents relating to their income and assets for some time, and to make them available to the administration when required. According to the French State, this right of the State to the communication of certain documents cannot be considered as an obstacle to the right to silence and to the prohibition against self-incrimination[106]. In the present case, the customs services did not summon Mr. Funke to confess to an offence or to provide proof of it himself; they simply asked him to give details of the items found by their agents, namely the bank statements that were discovered during the home visit of January 14, 1980[107].

The Commission reached the same conclusion as the French government[108]. Based mainly on the particularities of investigation procedures in economic and financial matters, in its view, neither the duty to produce bank statements nor the imposition of penalty payments were such as to undermine the principle of a fair trial.

The European Court of Human Rights concluded that there had been a violation of Article 6§1 of the Convention[109]. It considered that "the customs services provoked Mr. Funke's conviction in order to obtain certain documents, the existence of which they assumed, without having any certainty. Unable or unwilling to obtain them by any other means, they attempted to force the petitioner to provide proof of the offences committed. The particularities of customs law[110] could not justify such an infringement of the right of every accused person to remain silent and not to contribute to his/her own incrimination"[111]. The Court did not rule on the alleged violation of the second paragraph of article 6 but considered that the existence of a violation of the right not to incriminate oneself exempted him from examining the second ground, which is the presumption of innocence[112].

2.1.2 Murray ruling[113]

The *John Murray versus the United Kingdom ruling*, handed down by the European Court on February 8, 1996, is seen as the most important ruling in the "trilogy" studied. The case concerned the application of special legislation on the prevention of terrorism in Northern Ireland.

In this case, John Murray was arrested by the police on January 7, 1990, at 5:40 p.m. under section 14 of the Prevention of Terrorism Act 1989[114]. Pursuant to section 3 of the Northern Ireland Criminal Evidence Order 1988[115] the police warned him in the following terms:

> "You are not required to say anything unless you wish to do so; but I must warn you that if you fail to mention any fact which you will rely on in your defense in court, that failure to avail yourself of that opportunity may be taken by the court as corroborating evidence against you. If you wish to say something, your statement may be brought up as evidence."

At the time of the arrest, he was in a house in Belfast where a member of the Irish Republican Army, suspected of being an undercover member of the British police, was being held.

In response to the police warning, the petitioner indicated that he had nothing to say.

Upon arrival at the police station, the petitioner refused to identify himself to the police officer in charge of opening the police custody case file[116]. He was then informed of his right to tell a friend or relative about his detention but indicated that he opted to waive this right. A few moments later, he indicated that he wished to talk to a lawyer. He was denied this opportunity on the orders of a senior commissioner, allegedly under section 15(1) of the Northern Ireland Emergency Act 1987[117].

The denial of access to a lawyer was set at 48 hours from the start of the detention (i.e., January 7 from 5:40 p.m.). The chief commissioner explained this denial of the right to consult a lawyer as impeding the investigation of the acts of terrorism committed, and complicating operations to prevent another such act. A few hours later, a police officer asked the petitioner to explain his presence in the house where he had been arrested.[118] The officer warned the petitioner that if he did not do so, or if he refused to answer, a court, judge, or jury could draw conclusions from his refusal to speak, and those conclusions would appear to be legitimate[119]. After receiving a written copy of section 6 of the order[120], the petitioner said he had nothing to say.

John Murray was sentenced to eight years' imprisonment on the charge of aiding and abetting a member of the Irish Republican Army[121].

Before the commission of Inquiry, the petitioner alleged that the provisions of the 1988 order permitted an adverse inference to be drawn against the accused because he did not answer police questions or give evidence. He added that the use of this silence to conclude that he was guilty was contrary to Articles 6 § 1 and 6 § 2 of the European Convention[122]. He also complained that he had not been allowed to consult a lawyer during his detention[123].

The Government, for their part, argued that the issue was not whether the 1988 order was per se incompatible with the right to remain silent, but rather whether, in the circumstances of the case, the fact that conclusions had been drawn in accordance with Articles 4 and 6 thereof had tainted the criminal proceedings against the petitioner with unfairness, and responded with a nay since the order did not alter the burden of proof.

The Court reviewed this matter in the light of the law of evidence. Firstly, it reaffirmed the principle of the right to silence and its generalization to all criminal law. It did so in the following terms: "There is no doubt that, even if article 6 of the Convention does not expressly mention them, the right to remain silent during police questioning and the right not to contribute to one's own incrimination are generally recognized international norms, which are at the heart of the concept of a fair trial established in article 6. By protecting the accused from undue coercion by the authorities, these immunities help to avoid miscarriages of justice and ensure the result intended by Article 6[124].

This assertion places the right to silence at the heart of the concept of a fair trial.

Nevertheless, the Court places certain limits on this right. In this regard, the court specifies what the consequences, linked to the exercise of such a right, may be on the conviction: "the national court cannot find the defendant guilty simply because he/she choose to remain silent. It is only when the prosecution evidence calls for an explanation which the accused should be able to give; that the absence of an explanation may result in the conclusion, by simple common-sense reasoning, that there is no possible explanation and that the accused is guilty. Therefore, remaining silent from the beginning to the end of the proceedings may have certain consequences"[125].

It is therefore not possible to convict a person on the basis of his silence alone, but this silence can be taken into accounts for situations that demand an explanation, such that remaining silent from the beginning to the end of the proceedings may thus have consequences. In this case, the person concerned was able to remain silent without this being taken into consideration as an indication of guilt, the Court said.

Finally, the Court considered that it did not need to speculate on what would have actually happened if the petitioner had given statements to the police. The applicant had been advised and understood the meaning of the warning given to him, so that it was "neither unfair nor unreasonable" to draw conclusions from his attitude[126]. The Court therefore concluded that there had been no violation of Article 6 § 1 and 2. On the other hand, it found a violation of Article 6 § 3 with regard to the right of access to a lawyer[127].

2.1.3 Saunders ruling[128]

A few months after the *Murray ruling*, the European Court of Human Rights once again addressed the right to silence in the *Saunders v. United Kingdom ruling*, handed down by the Grand Chamber on December 17, 1996.

In this case, Mr. Ernest Saunders, a United Kingdom national, became Chairman and CEO of Guinness PLC, known as Guinness, in 1981[129].

In early 1986, Guinness was competing with another company, Argyll Group PLC, known as Argyll, for the takeover of a third company, Distillers Company PLC, known as Distillers. Guinness ultimately won the battle. Like Argyll's offer, Guinness' offer to Distillers shareholders included a substantial share exchange, and the prices at which Guinness and Argyll shares were listed on the London Stock Exchange were a decisive factor for both parties[130]. During the course of the raid, Guinness' share price rose dramatically, but once the unconditional offer was declared, there was a sharp and significant drop in its share price [131].

The significant increase in the price of Guinness shares listed on the stock exchange during the takeover bid was the result of an illegal share support operation. This involved certain individuals, known as supporters, who acquired shares in Guinness in order to maintain or inflate its listed shares[132]. In this scheme, the supporters received secret compensation for any losses they might suffer and, for some of them, huge fees if the Guinness bid was successful. These incentives were illegal for two reasons: firstly, they were not disclosed to the market in accordance with the City's takeover and merger code and secondly, they were not paid out of Guinness' own cash. This transaction is contrary to section 151 of the 1985 Companies Act, which prohibits a company from lending financial support to promote the purchase of its own shares[133].

The supporters who had acquired shares in the illegal share support operation were compensated and rewarded. In addition, some of the people who had helped to find supporters were able to obtain substantial bonuses in return. These too came from Guinness funds. In most cases, these payments were made by means of false invoices. These invoices concealed the illegal operation of supporting the shares. Allegations and rumors of wrongdoing during the raid eventually led the Minister of

Trade and Industry to appoint inspectors a few months after the events[134].

On January 12, 1987, the inspectors informed the Department of Trade and Industry (DTI) that they had physical evidence of criminal offenses. On the same day, the Department contacted Mr. John Wood at the Public Prosecutor's Office[135].

The petitioner was charged with the illegal stock support operation and was sent for trial to the Crown Court on April 27, 1989.

According to the petitioner, the use of the answers he gave to the inspectors of the Department of Trade and Industry at his trial automatically deprived the criminal proceedings of its fairness[136]. This argument was rejected by the Court of Appeal, which noted that in the 1985 Act, Parliament expressly and unequivocally provided that the answers given to the inspectors could be admitted as evidence in criminal proceedings, even if such admission violated the right not to contribute to one's own incrimination.

Before the European Commission of Human Rights, the applicant claimed that the statements he made under duress during the investigation were wrongly admitted as evidence against him in his subsequent criminal trial. In support of this claim, he argued that the Court's ruling, i.e., *Funke v. France and John Murray v. United Kingdom*, when referring to the right to a fair trial guaranteed by Article 6, encompasses the right to silence and the prohibition against self-incrimination[137].

According to the government, coercion could not and did not in itself deprive the proceedings of its fairness. Moreover, if the Court concluded that a particular response by Mr. Saunders could properly be considered self-incriminating, it was still necessary to assess whether the extremely limited use made of it was such as to deprive the criminal proceedings of its fairness. Such a deprivation was not apparent.

The Commission, on the other hand, considered that the right not to contribute to one's own incrimination is an important element of the protection of individuals against all kinds of pressure and coercion. This principle is linked to that of the presumption of innocence and must be applied equally to all types of accused, including those suspected of corporate fraud.

In this case, the elements that contributed to the conviction of the petitioner were derived from information that he himself was forced to provide. This information represented a significant part of the evidence against him at his trial. The use of this evidence put unacceptable pressure on Mr. Saunders and significantly impaired his ability to defend himself against the criminal charges against him. This contributed to depriving him of the opportunity to receive the fair trial guaranteed by Article 6 of the European Convention on Human Rights[138] The Commission therefore found a violation of Article 6 §1 of the Convention.

The European Court of Human Rights, following the Commission's reasoning, recalled that "even though article 6 of the Convention does not expressly mention it, the right to remain silent and the right not to contribute to one's own incrimination are generally recognized international norms, which are at the heart of the concept of a fair trial. One of the reasons for their existence is to protect the accused against undue coercion by the authorities. This right is closely linked to the principle of the presumption of innocence, established in Article 6 § 2 of the Convention"[139]. It adds that the right not to incriminate oneself primarily concerns the respect of the choice of an accused person to remain silent[140]. The Strasbourg court made another important clarification and said that the right not to incriminate oneself does not only extend to the use, in criminal proceedings, of data that could be obtained from the accused by means of coercive powers, but also to data that exist independently of the suspect's will. It cited, as examples, documents collected under warrant, the collection of breath, blood, urine, and body tissue samples for DNA analysis[141].

The Court went on to address the use of Saunders' statements in this case and asks whether there was an infringement of his right not to contribute to his own incrimination. In this case, during the administrative phase, Saunders had not made any self-incriminating statements, as he had not confessed his participation in the offences with which he was charged.

The Court will ultimately hold that, "in light of the notion of fairness established in Article 6, the right of the accused not to contribute to his own incrimination cannot reasonably be limited to confessions of wrongdoing or remarks directly implicating him/her. Statement obtained under duress, which at first appears to be non-incriminating, may subsequently be used in criminal proceedings to support the prosecution's case to contradict or cast doubt on accused person's other statements or to undermine his/her credibility. In the event that such evidence is submitted to a jury for consideration, the use of such testimony may prejudice the author. Therefore, it is the use that will be made, during the criminal trial, of the information gathered under duress that matters in this context"[142].

2.1.4 Lessons learned

This section focuses on the main lessons to be learned from the three case law decisions discussed in the previous sections.

It is apparent from the *Funke v. France* decision that the right to remain silent, if it includes the right to remain silent orally, also extends to the right not to produce documents against oneself[143]. This teaching of the Court has moreover been confirmed on several occasions[144]. It is also clear from this ruling that the right to silence is closely linked to the prohibition on the prosecuting authority to use coercion when trying to obtain evidence. This coercion is not exclusively physical but can also be moral. This was illustrated by the Funke ruling. The Court recognized that there was an obligation on the person concerned to provide certain information, with the consequence that there would be criminal sanctions against him if he refused to hand over the documents. However, as we have already explained, the right to silence and the prohibition against self-incrimination imply that the accused cannot be forced to incriminate himself. It is up to the prosecuting authority to gather sufficient evidence to establish the guilt of the accused.

In light of these contributions, a question caught our attention. In this case, the Strasbourg Court condemned France for violating Article 6 § 1 of the European Convention on Human Rights on the grounds that the customs administration had attempted to force the petitioner to provide evidence of offences he had allegedly committed (see above). The Court added that the particularities and requirements of customs law could not justify an infringement of the right to silence. Following this analysis by the Court, should it be concluded that the right to remain silent is an absolute right and that it should not be subject to any exception, even in the presence, in this case, of the particularities of customs law? In our view, the Court's analysis necessarily left such an interpretation open. The John Murray case finally provided an answer to this question (see below).

The conclusions drawn from *John Murray v. United Kingdom* are of particular interest to us since they address our original question. In fact, "the question at stake here is whether the exercise of the right to remain silent by an accused person could never be used to his/her disadvantage at trial or, in the alternative, whether it should always be considered improper coercion to inform him/her in advance that, under certain conditions, his/her silence could be used. In contrast to the Funke case law, the petitioner in this case remained silent. The question then arose as to the consequences of exercising this right.

The Court responded by stating on the one hand that it is not possible to conclude that the accused was convicted exclusively or essentially because he wanted to remain silent or refused to answer questions. On the other hand, it qualified this earlier statement [and thus limiting the right to silence] by arguing that it is "only when there is evidence [overwhelming charges[146]] which demands an explanation that the petitioner should be able to give; an absence of such explanation on his part being liable to lead to the conclusion, by simple **common sense** reasoning[147], that there is no possible explanation and that the accused is guilty."[148].

It concludes by stating that in determining whether drawing adverse inferences from the accused's silence violates section 6, one must consider:

1° the relevant circumstances

2° having regard in particular, where inferences can be drawn from the weight given to them by the national courts in assessing the evidence; and

3° the degree of coercion inherent in the situation.

It therefore follows from this case law that the right to remain silent is not an absolute right. However, we draw the reader's attention to the fact that some uncertainty and difficulty remain after this clarification posed by the *John Murray v. United Kingdom* case law. According to this case law, common sense seems to be the cursor, the dividing line whereon the judge should place him-/herself in order to determine whether, in a given situation, the silence maintained by the accused could lead to interpretations likely to spur a declaration of his/her guilt. However, common sense presupposes an ability to spontaneously discern the truth from falsehood, to appreciate things at their true value and to resolve, by rigorous reasoning, notions that are subject to all kinds of speculation[149]. As a result, the concept seems difficult to grasp, at least from a legal standpoint. The difficulty of this solution lies precisely in the fluctuating and volatile nature of a notion, which is marked by subjectivity. It seems to us that this term hinders respect for legal certainty, in that the absence of guidelines [or simply of a legal definition] of the concept makes it subject to all sorts of loopholes and uncertainties. This could have the direct consequence of encouraging arbitrariness, and of giving the silence of the person who chooses to exercise his right various and varied interpretations, subject to the interpretation of the "common sense" of the judge who is called upon to render his judgment.

Finally, *Saunders v. United Kingdom* teaches us that self-incrimination will not be limited solely to the admission of an offence[150]. It is necessary to consider the case in question and to examine whether the use made of the contentious statement before the criminal court favors the incrimination of the person concerned. The fact that the prosecution may use the coerced statement of an accused person, in order to contradict and cast doubt on or undermine his credibility, must be considered self-incriminating. Finally, as mentioned in this judgment, the right against self-incrimination does not only extend in criminal proceedings to data that can be obtained from the accused through the use of coercive powers, but also to those that exist independently of the will of the accused[151].

2.2 Strasbourg case law: analysis of four judgments of the European Court of Human Rights establishing the right to silence

Following the three founding judgments, a series of judgments of the European Court of Human Rights have since been handed down, refining, clarifying, or developing the foundations of the case law developed (see above). Given the rich contribution of these cases, we felt it necessary to "complete" our previous reasoning with the lessons learned from these later judgments. Four case law decisions will be examined in this section.

2.2.1 William and Karen Condron v. United Kingdom[152]

Mr. William Condron is an Irish national and Mrs. Karen Condron is a British national[153]. They both admitted to being heroin addicts[154]. They lived in a large low-cost housing estate in South London[155]. Mr. James Curtis, their neighbor, was involved in the case in which they were implicated[156]. All three were prosecuted for similar offenses, namely the supply of heroin and possession of heroin with intent to supply. According to the prosecution, the petitioners prepared packets of heroin and passed them on to their neighbor, James Curtis, so that he could sell them[157]. Some police recordings made between April 24 and 28, 1995, revealed the transmission of heroin by Mr. and Mrs. Condron to Mr. James Curtis, as well as the subsequent transmission to other individuals. On April 28, 1995, the Condrons were arrested[158]. Sixteen packets of heroin were found in their apartment.

On April 29, 1995, the Condron couple were questioned by the police[159]. Their lawyer, Mr. Delbourgo, noted that his clients were in a state of craving and could not participate in the police interrogation. However, the medical examiner, after examining them, did not come to the same conclusion. According to the medical examiner, although he recognized being in the presence of drug addicts with signs and symptoms of craving, this was not sufficient to prevent the interrogation from taking place. The doctor explained his reasoning by mentioning the fact that they were clear-minded and able to answer the questions[160].

Having questioned them separately and in the presence of their lawyer, the police informed the petitioners using the following words:

> "You are not obliged to say anything, however, you must note that your defense may be weakened if during your interrogation you do not mention something that you will later invoke in court. What you say may be used against you."

They stated that they understood the warning and refused to answer only one question, the one regarding the discovery of the sixteen packets of heroin. More precisely, the petitioners answered "no comment"[161] to this question.

The petitioners' trial took place from the 16 October to 2 November 1995 before a jury in the Kingston Crown Court[162]. On the question of whether the Cordons were unfit for police interrogation, the judge agreed with the doctor's observations and concluded that their lawyer had wrongly considered them unfit for questioning. In doing so, he decided to attach the minutes of the interviews to the file.

During the trial, the petitioners explained that the heroin that was found in their apartment was for their personal use. When questioned about the incident recorded on April 26, 1995, they provided additional explanations, which they had not given to the police during their interrogation.

The Condrons were convicted of possession of heroin with intent to supply[163]. In their petition to the European Commission of Human Rights, the petitioners alleged that they had been deprived of their right to a fair trial because the trial judge had allowed the jury to draw inferences against them from their silence during police questioning.

This case bears important similarities to the *John Murray v. United Kingdom* ruling (see above). In reaching its decision, the Court reiterated the principles of that earlier case law in order to avoid departing from it. In Murray, the Court emphasized that the silence of an accused in situations that clearly call for an explanation may be taken into consideration when assessing the strength of the evidence against him, provided that adequate safeguards were respected[164].

In this case, the Condron couple expressed their reasons for refusing to provide explanations during the interrogation[165]. According to the Court, however, the trial judge drew the jury's attention to this explanation "in terms that left the jurors free to draw conclusions against them[166]. It added that fairness required that the jury be told that they could draw inferences against the petitioners only if they were satisfied that, in this case, the petitioners' silence could reasonably be attributed to the fact that they had no answers to give when questioned[167]. Furthermore, in the circumstances of this case, it was a jury that was called upon to decide on the guilt and not a professional judge. This made it all the more important to ensure that the jury was properly instructed as to how it might interpret the silence of the petitioners[168].

It was clear from the study of this case law that it is possible to draw adverse inferences from the silent attitude of the litigant. However, this can only be done in particular circumstances[169], and with all due caution[170]. In this case, however, the jury was not properly informed[171]. For these reasons, the Court found a violation of Article 6 § 1 of the Convention.

2.2.2 Liam Averill v. United Kingdom[172]

The Liam Averill case came less than a month after the Condron ruling. In this case, Mr. Liam Averill was arrested a few hours after a double murder suspected to have been carried out as part of terrorist actions by the Irish Republican Army. From his hair, fibers that might have come from a balaclava were collected[173]. The police officer who questioned him about this previously warned him of his rights using the following words:

> "You are not required to say anything unless you wish to; but I must warn you that if you fail to mention any fact which you will rely upon in your defense in court, such failure to avail yourself of this opportunity may be taken by the court as corroborating evidence against you. If you wish to say something, your statement may be introduced as evidence".

During this interrogation, Mr. Averill decided not to answer any of the questions[174]. He was therefore not allowed to have a lawyer present during his initial questioning.

The trial judge convicted the petitioner mainly on the basis of forensic evidence. The judge also found "highly unfavorable findings" against the petitioner because he had not answered any of the questions asked during the interrogations, nor had he provided any other explanation, including about the fibers found in his hair and clothing[175]. This decision was upheld by the appeal judge. In this case, the decision of the European Court of Human Rights was that there was no violation of the right to a fair trial since the petitioner was not convicted by the trial judge solely on the basis of his silence. His sentence was the result of several elements that contributed to his conviction[176]. In explaining this reasoning, however, it pointed out that warning the petitioner that his silence may lead to adverse consequences involves a certain degree of indirect coercion[177]. It qualified this by stating that this element alone is not decisive[178].

It added that the possibility of drawing unfavorable conclusions from the silence of an accused person must be limited[179].

Its explanation continued with this statement: "While in most cases an innocent person is expected to be willing to cooperate with the police by explaining that he or she did not participate in the offences charged, a person may have reasons in a given case for not wanting to do so. They may find it more appropriate to remain silent until they have the opportunity to consult a lawyer. Therefore, great caution must be exercised in giving weight to the silence of a person who is asked to testify while denied access to counsel. In such circumstances, it cannot be entirely excluded that the persistent silence of the accused is based on the sound advice he or she may have received from his or her absent lawyer.

Nor does the need for caution in interpreting silence disappear simply because an accused is finally allowed to see his lawyer and still refuses to answer questions, the Court said"[180].

This opinion has earned the Court several harsh criticisms. In this regard, we mention the criticism of the doctrine authors Cuykens, Holzapfel and Kennes who considered this opinion to be "risky"[181]. In their words, "the Court, by such statements, supports the idea that silence is the prerogative of the guilty party who intends to conceal his or her involvement in the commission of an offense. Silence should therefore be interpreted by the judge to see whether the choice of the accused cannot be linked to an exceptional situation, compatible with the hypothesis of the innocence of the accused"[182]. On this point, our opinion differed greatly. This assessment by the Court seems to us to be more than relevant. This parallelism between the absence of the lawyer during an interrogation, the refusal of the defendant to testify and the prohibition, in such cases, of speculating on the interpretation to be given to the silence of the person who is invoking it, explains it.

We now know that when a suspect deprived of his liberty is denied access to a lawyer, as in this case, if he/she makes self-incriminating statements and these are used by the trial judge against him, article 6 of the European Convention on Human Rights is irremediably violated[183]. The Court's assessment therefore highlights the importance of the lawyer during the interrogation. Indeed, the lawyer's role during the interrogation is not negligible, as he/she is present to remind the accused of his rights [including the right to remain silent] and to ensure that the guarantees granted to him are not violated. We maintain that this statement by the Court can thus usefully justify that an individual, who is accused of serious offences, simply chooses to remain silent without this concealing a desire to opt for a defense strategy designed to hide his guilt.

2.2.3 Thomas Telfner v. Austria[184]

This case involves an individual and a driver[185]. After being hit by a vehicle and slightly injured, the victim took note of the driver's license plate number before the driver fled the scene[186]. The police authorities, after finding the owner of the vehicle, went to his home; it was the mother of Mr. Thomas Telfner. The latter indicated that she had not driven a vehicle on the date of the events, specifying that the vehicle was used by several members of the family, including her daughter who was present and her son who was absent[187]. It emerged from the investigations that the main user of the vehicle in question was Thomas Telfner[188]. He was summoned to the police station for a hearing but did not show up[189]. He was prosecuted and in court, without providing the slightest explanation, he was convicted of involuntary assault and battery in the first and second degree[190]. The national judges established his guilt, in particular because he had refused to speak to the police when asked to do so.

Thomas Telfner appealed to the European Court of Human Rights, basing his application on the violation of article 6 paragraph 2 of the Convention, i.e., the principle of presumption of innocence. The right to silence was not invoked here, but the Court nevertheless based its decision on the *Murray v. United Kingdom* case law. As in Murray, the Court considered whether there might be a presumption of guilt in certain cases, so that an accused person would be obliged to take an active stance in his trial, by providing clarification of what he had done at the time of the alleged offences[191]. In addition, still referring to Murray case law, the Court recalled having admitted that unfavorable judgment had been taken against the accused because of his silence, but only after considerations[192]. On the one hand, there must be significant procedural guarantees, and on the other hand, the evidence against the accused must be overwhelming[193]. In the current case, the Court found that there was no such evidence to require that such an explanation be provided for Thomas Telfner. The Court therefore concluded that there had been a violation of Article 6 §2 of the Convention.

We consider this judgment to be of major importance. It highlights the link between the presumption of innocence and the right to silence[194] (*see* point 1.2. above).

2.2.4 Keith Beckles v. United Kingdom[195]

Mr. Mohamoud accompanied a prostitute to his apartment to have sex with her[196]. There, other people were allegedly present, including Keith Beckles. They allegedly stripped her and pushed her out of the fourth-floor window of the apartment[197]. None of the occupants of the apartment called for help.

Keith Beckles was subsequently interviewed by the police and was told the following:

> "You are not required to say anything unless you wish to; but if you fail to mention any fact which you will rely on in your defense in court, that omission may be sustained by the court as corroborating incriminating evidence. If you wish to say something, your statement can be introduced as evidence."

Prior to his attorney's arrival, Mr. Beckles made some statements through which he explained that the victim was not pushed but jumped on her own. However, following his lawyer's advice, he changed his attitude and said he did not want to say anything more[198].

At the end of the trial, the judge instructed the jury on questions of law, including how they could interpret the accused's silence during the hearing. The judge further instructed the jury that they could draw adverse inferences from the accused's silence if it appeared to them to be fair and proper in light of the facts of the case (i.e., the fact that during his trial, Mr. Beckles did not discuss the reasons for his presence in the apartment on the night that gave rise to the events in question)[199].

In this case, the Court found a violation of the right to a fair trial. It considered that the explanations given by the judge to the jury obscured the credibility of the explanations given by the petitioner. According to the Court, the judge failed to specify that the few explanations given, which served as a basis for the decision, were given before the meeting between the accused and his counsel. The Court had already explained the importance it attaches to the presence of counsel when statements obtained by the accused are used against him/her (see above). In addition, the judge invited the jury to consider whether the reasons given by the accused in deciding to remain silent were legitimate reasons, without adding that this unfavorable interpretation must have only possible ensued from his guilt[200].

In the Court's view, the discretionary power of the jury should have been limited to ensure that it was exercised in a manner that is in line with the right to silence[201]. The jury should have been asked to be more cautious in considering the silence of the accused, especially when it was acknowledged that the applicant had refused to answer questions under the advice of his lawyer[202].

2.2.5 Lessons learned[203]

In the end, we conclude from this line of case laws that, although the right to silence and the right not to contribute to one's own incrimination are internationally recognized procedural guarantees and concepts at the heart of a fair trial (see above), withholding adverse consequences from the right of the accused to remain silent does not *ipso facto* entail a violation of the right to a fair trial guaranteed by Article 6 of the European Convention on Human Rights. In fact, as the judgments considered in this section have shown, when a case concerning the right to silence is brought before the Court, the Court makes a point of examining the reasons why the person concerned has decided to remain silent[204].

This is particularly true when the accused justifies his silence by the absence of a lawyer during his interrogation[205]. The Court is also interested in examining the reasons why the accused chose to remain silent.

As for the issue of whether negative conclusions can be drawn from the silence of the accused, the Strasbourg case law remains constant on this issue: it is not possible to convict an individual exclusively on the basis of his or her silence or refusal to answer questions or to give evidence[206]. Silence could at most be considered as an element that corroborates the evidence, but not the ultimate reason for the conviction[207]. This was the case in John Murray (see above) and Liam Averill (see above), such that in these cases the probative value of the other evidence against the accused were already considered "overwhelming". Therefore, interpreting the silence of the person concerned in a situation that certainly calls for explanation as corroborating evidence of guilt does not entail a violation or disregard of the right to remain silent[208].

It is considered that understanding the exercise of silence in this way makes it vulnerable. Indeed, although the European Court of Human Rights, through its case laws maintains that it is in principle not possible to have recourse to silence alone to motivate the decision of guilt of the accused, the exercise of this right could nevertheless be, in particular circumstances, an element that corroborates the evidence against the accused.

In addition, two criticisms still seem important to us. The first involves the requirements formulated by the case law of the European Court of Human Rights when it comes to understanding the right to silence by the national courts; these requirements are sometimes ignored by the Court itself, and are difficult to implement in legal systems like that of Belgium[209].

In several judgments, when confronted with a case in which the person concerned has asserted his/her right to silence, the Court itself refers to silence as prima facie evidence, even when the overwhelming charges are not found[210]. In so doing, it gives silence the weight that it nevertheless forbids in its case law to give it and becomes guilty of the error that it condemns.

The second criticism concerns what prevails in Belgian law. When referring to the procedural guarantees that must be observed, the Court requires that the person concerned be informed of the legal consequences of his or her possible silence as soon as he or she is notified of this right[211]. However, in Belgian law, the legal provisions that set out this right do not mention all the details (for example, there is no mention in the Belgian legal provision of the right of the accused to remain silent, simply that he/she cannot be forced to accuse him-/herself) of the possible consequences to which the person exercising it is exposed[212]. It should also be added that this right is not generally presented as a fundamental right or a procedural guarantee that should not be neglected[213].

This reality makes it difficult for the litigant to become aware of this procedural guarantee and of the real consequences that may arise from its application. It is one thing to remain silent, but it is also necessary to know why and how to do so, as we have mentioned in our previous comments (see 1.3).

The analysis of the right to silence in the Strasbourg case law has enabled us to draw some major lessons regarding this right. We now turn to the establishment of the right to silence and the prohibition of self-incrimination in three different countries in order to answer our initial question, which, as we recall, is whether silence can motivate a decision of guilt in England, Belgium, and the United States.

3. Establishment of the right to silence in England, the United States and Belgium

In order to determine whether the silence of the accused can motivate a decision of guilt in England, Belgium, and the United States, let us now turn to the three legal orders mentioned above and to the response that each of them gives to our initial question.

3.1 England[214]

3.1.1 The right to silence in the British legal system

There is a right to silence and a prohibition against self-incrimination in the English legal system. Indeed, the right to silence is a tradition that England has recognized since the 17th century. The existence of this right is attributed to Judge Edward Coke, who was known for his strong opposition to the practice of the ecclesiastical courts[215].

It is necessary to go back to the beginning of the sixteenth century to understand the reasoning that led to the existence of this right in the British tradition[216]. At that time, alongside the *common law* courts and tribunals, other jurisdictions called the *Court of Chancery*[217]. were developed. These courts were mainly ecclesiastical. Those brought before them were obliged to take an oath, even though they had no knowledge of the charges against them. This practice was not without consequences. First, it meant that individuals who refused to take the oath would be liable to a *contempt of court*[218] Secondly, if these individuals dared to lie, they were guilty [which is a mortal sin in the ecclesiastical court]. Thirdly, if they finally decided to accept the charges brought against them, they were accusing themselves and were guilty of a violation of their natural right to self-preservation. They were thus seen as offending the person of God the Creator Himself.

Judge Edward Coke was the first to banish this deadly trialogue by saying that any speech by which the litigant incriminates himself could not be received in the courts. The Common Law also adopted this position, which was the set off point for the tradition of the right to silence in England. Since then, the right to remain silent has even been recognized as a central right in the British legal system[219].

In England, the recognition of the right to silence and the prohibition against self-incrimination as recognized by the *common* law does not mean that there is no legal obligation to speak to the police or even to provide evidence in court. What this right implies is that there should be no disadvantage to the defendant in refusing either to cooperate with the police or to testify[220]. This right is therefore not only embodied in the possibility of the accused not to incriminate him-/herself, but in "the prohibition of the courts from affirming or asserting, either by the judges or by the prosecuting authority, to conclude that a person is guilty merely because he/she has refused to respond to allegations, particularly those of the police, or has refused to give evidence at the hearing in the interests of his own defense"[221].

Looking at the manifestation of the right to silence in British law requires a distinction between two periods. Firstly, there is the period preceding the coming into force of the *Criminal Justice and Public Order Act*, and then the period after their enforcement[222]. Until 1995, when the *Criminal Justice and Public Order Act* came into force, a suspect, being interrogated by the police, was made to know of the right to silence[223]. The content of this right is determined by the following rules:

a) Answers to police questions shall not be admitted as evidence unless they were given voluntarily without oppression or inducement of any kind[224].
b) An accused may testify at his own trial if and only if he chooses to do so[225].
c) Only limited statements may be made if a person chooses to exercise his or her right to silence[226].
d) No inference of guilt should be drawn solely from the person's exercise of his/her right to silence[227].

As for the wording of the warning to the litigant/accused to make him/her aware of this right, it was formulated as follows: "You do not have to say anything unless you wish to do so, but what you say may be given in evidence"[228]. According to Lord Diplock, this warning is a reminder to the litigant of a right, recognized by the *common law*, to which he or she may have recourse for protection. However, since the *Criminal Justice and Public Order Act* came into force, this warning has been modified by the reform of the law of evidence. The right to silence, which was not spared, is now issued in these terms: "you do not have to say anything. But it may harm your defense if you do not mention, when interrogated, something which you later rely on in court. Anything you do say may be used as an evidence"[229]. The consequence of this new wording is no less important since it tends to encourage the accused to speak preferably to the police rather than to remain silent. In fact, by this reworded warning, the person is now warned that it is in his or her interest to present his or her defense immediately, at the risk of seeing this same defense called into question at the hearing[230].

It seemed to us that even though the search for greater efficiency in the English criminal justice system was the driving force behind these reforms, the fact remains that the right to silence has been altered to such an extent that it is questionable whether it is really effective. "In the end, is this right not more of a risk taken by the person being questioned?"[231].

3.1.2 The right to silence during police interrogation vs. the right to silence at the hearing

To understand the right to silence during police interrogation, we must look at section 34 of the *Criminal Justice and Public Order Act*. It refers to the fate of facts not mentioned by the accused during the police interrogation but mentioned by the latter during the trial. In such circumstances, it will be possible to draw adverse "inferences"[232] from the silence of the accused, at least with respect to the absence of an explanation of certain facts during his or her interrogation[233]. What section 34 of the aforementioned act provides is that in order to draw inferences from the silence of the accused in relation to facts that concern his hearing, it will be necessary to verify whether the fact(s) for which he has opted for his right to remain silent is (are) in fact related to his defense. In addition, it will be important to analyze the reasons why he/she did not mention these facts during his interrogation[234]. This section 34 may also apply when the accused presents a version at the hearing that is contradictory to that which he/she presented during the police interrogation.

However, these discrepancies do not necessarily have to lead to the justification of particular conclusions. This situation will have to be analyzed on a case-by-case basis[235].

As for the understanding of silence during the hearing, before section 35 of the Criminal Justice and Public Order Act was enacted, it was prohibited to comment, during the trial, on the accused's failure to testify.

Therefore, the examination had to be preceded by a warning that the accused was not required to answer any questions put to him or her, and that his or her silence could not be taken at trial as evidence of guilt. This regulation in England was explained by the old rule that courts and tribunals were already obliged to reject all confessions obtained by coercion and oppression.

However, since the introduction of section 35 of the *Criminal Justice and Public Order Act*[236], the judge and/or jury may now use the silence of the accused as evidence when the latter refuses to speak at trial. However, this is subject to the condition wherein the accused's silence is maintained without serious reasons to justify his or her choice of silence[237]. In this sense, the case law of *R. v. Burdett*[238] sets out the possibility of using silence as evidence of guilt when the defense fails to explain a situation that requires explanation. This power is not absolute and must be qualified. In R. v. Rhodes, the judge commented on the silence of the accused.

According to the Court of Appeal, it is possible to comment on the silence of an accused and to draw consequences therefrom. However, it specifies that the use of this silence to spur guilt is conditional. There are certain circumstances that call for the judge to refrain from commenting on the silence of the accused" the Court stated[239].

These particular conditions, which must be observed in order to draw adverse inferences from the silence of the accused, are themselves set out in section 35 of the *Criminal Justice and Public Order Act*:

1. The accused must have entered a plea of not guilty;
2. The accused must be physically and mentally fit to testify

3. The accused must have been warned of his or her right to testify and of the fact that inferences may be drawn from his or her failure to testify or to answer questions; and the accused must have failed to testify or, while testifying, have refused, without substantial cause, to answer questions.

It remains to be clarified that even if the judge and/or jury may draw inferences from the silence of the accused during the trial, the latter could not be convicted on this basis alone[240]. Section 38(3) of the Criminal Justice and Public Order Act 1994 expressly states: *"A person shall not have the proceedings against him transferred to the Crown Court for trial, have a case to answer or be convicted of an offence solely on an inference drawn from such a failure or refusal as is mentioned in section 34 (2), 35 (2) or 37 (2)"*[241]. The English judge may draw inferences from the silence of the accused but may not base his or her verdict on this element alone, as the European Court of Human Rights reminded us in its ruling on *Condron v. United Kingdom* (see above)[242].

3.2 The United States

Before beginning our discussion of the United States, a few terminological clarifications must be made.

- **The grand jury**[243] is a pillar of the American judicial system. According to the Fifth Amendment of the US Constitution, this grand jury must intervene in all criminal cases tried at the federal level to decide on the basis of the evidence presented by the prosecutor, whether or not to hold a trial. It is composed of 16 to 23 citizens chosen by lot. It is convened at the request of the prosecutor and is endowed by the most extensive investigative powers. It can thus hear, on its own initiative or at the request of the prosecutor, any person concerned by the case it is investigating.
- More reference will be made to the **privilege against self-incrimination** [rather than the right to silence], as this is the term commonly used in American legal literature.

3.2.1 Miranda v. Arizona[244]

In 1966, the case that gave rise to *Miranda v. Arizona* confronted American judges with the question of when the confession of a litigant/accused would be admissible as evidence in a criminal case against him/her. This case is one of the most emblematic cases on the issue of the right to silence in the United States. It was in this case that the precise contours of the right to silence, the privilege against self-incrimination, and the right to have counsel present during police interrogation were affirmed.

In this case, in Phoenix, Arizona, a girl who was 18 years old at the time of the incident was walking home. An individual stopped her and forced her into his vehicle[245]. He took her out of the city and raped her before driving her back to a few blocks to her home. Later, Ernesto Miranda was found thanks to the registration number of the vehicle which the victim had recognized and described to the police a few days after the crime. Ernesto was arrested at his home on March 13, 1963 and placed in police custody[246]. During his interrogation by the police, Ernesto Miranda denied any involvement in the rape of the young girl[247]. He was then presented to the victim, during a police-organized eyewitness identification procedure, alongside three other men of Latin American origin. He was the only one wearing glasses and a t-shirt. The victim does not identify him formally but specifies that he is the one who resembles the most his aggressor.

Later, Miranda will be interviewed without a lawyer present[248]. He then filled out a form in which he stated that he made a voluntary, non-coerced statement and will write a written confession in which he admits to being the perpetrator of the sexual assault in question. He reiterated this orally and also confessed to other incriminating acts committed several months earlier[249].

Ernesto Miranda was then assisted by a court-appointed lawyer. The latter pointed out the irregularity of the confession and the police interrogation. He argued that during the cross-examination, Miranda had not been informed of his right to counsel, nor had he been warned that anything he said could be used against him in a court of law[250]. He also added that his client had not confessed voluntarily, but that the confession had been obtained under some form of coercion, which tainted the procedure with several irregularities. The argument was rejected by the judge. Miranda was found guilty[251].

Believing that his client had been deprived of his rights under the U.S. Constitution (5th and 6th amendments[252]), the lawyer did not stop there and decided to appeal to the Supreme Court of the State of Arizona, which, in April 1965, confirmed the first decision.

The case was later taken up by an activist lawyer who was a member of the American Civil Liberties Union[253]. The latter saw in this case a major constitutional question that could have a considerable impact on the rights of the defense.

It was in this context that the case came before the US Supreme Court. The majority standpoints reversed the Arizona Supreme Court's decision, holding that the police custody was coercive, and that the confession was inadmissible because Miranda had not been informed of his rights beforehand (the right not to testify against oneself and the right to counsel).

It was in this decision that the court established the "Miranda Right" contained in the Miranda Warnings. This warning reads as follows: *"You have the right to remain silent. If you give up this right, anything you say can and will be used against you in a court of law. You have the right to an attorney and to have an attorney present during questioning. If you cannot afford an attorney, one will be provided to you free of charge. During each interrogation, you may decide at any time to invoke these rights, not to answer any questions or make any statements"*[254]. Ernesto Miranda was retried without reference to his written confession.

The verdict as to his guilt will remain unchanged[255].

The above-mentioned warning carries with it the consecration of the right to silence from the very first words of its formulation. It follows from the Miranda case law that if the person being questioned invokes his or her right to silence after receiving the Miranda warning, the questioning must cease. However, if the individual chooses to speak with knowledge of his or her rights, what he or she says may well be used against him or her.

An important clarification remains; police officers must use precise, clear, and simple expressions in order to convey this right to the individual in the most optimal manner. A clear warning will allow voluntary statements resulting from the interrogation to be admissible. On the contrary, a warning without clarity will not have the same effect. One thing is certain, the frequent use and adaptation of "Miranda Warnings" in American television soap operas[256] makes it almost impossible for the litigant/accused to argue ignorance of its existence. However, the duty to bring these rights to the attention of the litigant lies with the police and the lawyer, and not with the film industry, no matter how enthusiastically it has taken up the formula.

We now know which events gave rise to the famous Miranda Warnings in the United States, the symbol of the right to silence and the prohibition against self-incrimination in the United States. Let us now look at the place reserved for the right to silence in the American criminal justice system. Silence is a constitutional right in the United States, "The Fifth" as it is commonly called by Americans.

3.2.2 The Fifth Amendment to the US Constitution and the privilege against self-incrimination (*The Fifth*) [257]

In the United States, the right to silence enjoys a special position because it has a constitutional basis. The Fifth Amendment of the American Constitution guarantees the accused protection against self-incrimination, which is implemented by the accused's recourse to his/her right to silence[258]. This explains why the American litigant wishing to take refuge behind his/her right to silence will do so through the expression "I plead the fifth"[259]. The Fifth Amendment reads as follows: **"[...] No person shall be compelled to testify against him-/herself in a criminal trial."**[260].

A plurality of objectives underlies the constitution of the above-mentioned privilege. In the United States, where the right to silence is constitutionalized, "there is a desire to equalize the balance of power between the individual and the state, which is endowed with *overwhelming force*[261]. There is also a desire to preserve the integrity of the justice system[262]. The protection afforded by this amendment is in a context where the search for the truth should not lead to the conviction of a person who is not guilty[263]. The idea behind this assertion was that the guilty should not escape and the non-guilty should not suffer[264]. The Twining v. New Jersey ruling confirms this assertion by stating that the protection offered by the privilege against self-incrimination is primarily intended to prevent wrongful convictions[265].

As for the appearance of the privilege, it should be noted that it did not appear with the creation of the Fifth Amendment[266]. The privilege was first observed in most of the constitutions of the former American colonies before there was a need to recognize it in the American Bill of Rights[267].

As for the scope of the privilege, it limited to statements that are incriminating to the litigant in question. The privilege does not protect against giving false testimony[268], nor does it allow an accused to hide behind his or her silence in order to refuse to answer questions put to him/her. The accused may well be compelled to answer all types of questions put to him or her[269]. He/she may well be compelled to answer questions relating to his/her private life, provided that they are not of such a nature as to incriminate him-/herself. The lessons learned from *Hale v. Henkel* and *Counselman v. Hitchock* reiterate this. They make it clear that the Fifth Amendment is intended to protect only against self-incriminating statements[270]. The fact that an answer may damage the reputation of the accused is not, therefore, a sufficient ground for invoking this protection through silence[271].

3.2.3 The possibility of drawing inferences from silence in American law

The question of interest to us in this section is whether, under American law, it is possible to draw inferences from the silence of the accused when the latter has recourse to the protection offered by the Fifth Amendment. In other words, could the exercise of the privilege motivate the conviction of the person exercising it?

We will answer this question by citing cases from American jurisprudence on this issue.

The Doyle v. Ohio ruling teaches us that it would be inconsistent to inform the accused of his/her right to silence and then use that silence against him/her[272]. *Wilson v. United States* ruling states that the use of the Fifth Amendment may not be commented on, or lead to adverse inferences, such that jurors ought not be influenced by it[273]. The *Griffin v. California* ruling confirms that the accused's silence cannot be commented on by the judge since it could attract the attention of the jury and lead them to use it in evidence against the accused[274]. In Carter v. Kentucky, the Court revisited the issue and made a further clarification regarding the attitude of the jury. It said that the prohibition from commenting on the accused's failure to testify should not prevent a judge from telling the jury that they cannot draw adverse inferences from silence[275]. Indeed the 5th Amendment requires that instructions prohibiting adverse inferences from the accused's silence be directed to the jury, for in the absence of such instructions, the court continues, it will be possible for the jury to draw inferences from that silence.

From all of the above cases, the policy answer seems to be clear: it is not possible to draw inferences from the accused's silence when he/she invokes the Fifth Amendment. Indeed, the person who invokes the protection of the Fifth Amendment is only benefiting from a right that is legally recognized, "therefore, even if the accused had refused to speak to the authorities because of his guilt, it would be difficult to attribute meaning to the silence, since, in fact, his silence is explained by the exercise of this constitutionalized privilege"[276].

A major clarification remains to be made in order to complete the lessons provided on this point. In American law, there is, at the hearing, a total right to silence for the accused[277]. However, if the latter finally wishes to take a stance in the debate, and break his/her silence, he will be obliged to take an oath at the hearing and swear "to tell the truth and nothing but the truth"[278]. Thus, he/she will become a kind of witness in his/her own case[279].

3.3 Belgium

In this section devoted to the right to silence in Belgian law, we will not dwell on the outlines (i.e., definition, basis of the right to silence) since this was dealt with in the first chapter. We will deal with the manifestation of the right to silence in Belgian law, and more particularly with the question of the possibility of using this silence to motivate the decision of guilt. In order to answer this question, we found it interesting to look at the case law of the Belgian Court of Cassation.

In Belgian law, there are many opinions on the right to silence. Some authors present themselves as fervent defenders of the right to silence. In this posture, they propose an analysis that calls for caution because of the existence of elements likely to weaken this right. In this regard, Philippe Carré, in his observations, maintained that there is, in the use of the right to silence, a risk that silence may induce "in view of and according to the prior knowledge that the investigating judge has of the case file"[280]. He added that this right risks becoming "illusory by the mere fact that, psychologically, the refusal to explain is tantamount to a confession [of guilt], of non-contestation of the charges brought, or at least of a desire to conceal a truth that is about to be revealed"[281]. Others, however, such as Christian De Valkeneer, are not so enthusiastic when it comes to this right. According to Mr. De Valkeneer, "while it is true that silence alone cannot constitute evidence leading to a conviction, it is a real clue which, combined with other elements, can lead to such a result"[282].

In our view, this second observation strongly undermines the right to silence and the right against self-incrimination, in such a way that all other subsequent oral claims by the person invoking this right will be annihilated. This view contributes to making the right to silence, if not an exclusive basis for conviction, a key indicator of guilt. From then on, the right to remain silent is no longer a prerogative recognized to the person who considers it useful to use it as part of his or her defense strategy, but the element that will lead to interpreting the slightest blink, the slightest word, or the slightest attitude to the detriment of the presumed innocent. This would be tantamount to undermining the fundamental principle of the presumption of innocence, to deprive the rights of the defense of their substance, and yet "the defense must be free; this is a principle of public order"[283]. Our reasoning echoes that of Judge Edmond Pettiti, who considered that "the right to silence is a major principle. Any constraint that has the effect of penalizing the exercise of this right constitutes an infringement of this principle"[284].

In Belgian law, the case law of the Court of Cassation is more in line with the thesis that "the judge cannot draw any negative conclusions from silence"[285] and that it is important to "proscribed with the utmost energy, the attitude of certain judges who infer, from this adopted defense strategy, any unfavorable argument on which they base a conviction"[286].

Thus, silence alone is not in itself evidence of guilt. The trial judge, if he wishes to interpret the silence of the accused, must seek to interpret his/her motive of being silent[287].

The Court of Cassation, in a decision rendered on April 5, 2000, considered that "a violation of the rights of the defense, of which the right to silence is a part, cannot be established by the sole fact that the trial judge, after having listed the evidence against the accused, notes, on the one hand, that the latter systematically refused to give the necessary explanations and, on the other hand, that all of the elements of the case are of such a nature as to create the conviction that the charge has been established"[288]. In this case, several elements, including silence, were such as to lead the judge to establish the guilt of the accused[289]. The taking into consideration of silence was therefore not the exclusive element in establishing the guilt of the accused[290]. There is therefore no infringement of the right to silence.

On October 5, 2010, the Court confirmed this principle, considering that "the right to silence does not imply that the judge could never draw conclusions from the silence of the accused and does not prevent this inference, without being general, from being made in the light of the concrete circumstances; on this condition, the judge may consider a silence that is significant according to the factual circumstances, accompanied by other evidence, as incriminating evidence"[291]. The Court of Cassation, in a case in which the defendant had provided information to the authorities in the absence of a lawyer, did not fail to find a violation of article 6 of the European Convention on Human Rights[292]. It considered that these statements could not be used in concluding on the credibility of the case[293]. By doing this it endorsed the view that statements made in contravention of the right to silence and the prohibition against self-incrimination cannot be used to establish the credibility of the case[294].

In the end, there are many decisions of the Belgian Court of Cassation[295] which illustrate that the court agrees with the teachings of the case law of the European Court of Human Rights (see 1.2.4. and 4.2.5.) by adopting the developments of the Strasbourg Court.

However, one major clarification remains to be made. Whether Belgian case law refuses to have exclusive recourse to silence to spur the decision of guilt of the accused, there is nothing that guarantees that the accused's continued silence will not contribute to increasing the likelihood or him/her being convicted; the opposite is moreover true[296].

After having studied the particularities of each of the three countries studied, we shall now proceed to a cross-sectional analysis which will enable us to bring out the common and contradictory elements, before finally turning to two topical cases relevant to our study topic.

4. Cross-sectional analysis and topical cases

While the Belgian, British, and American legal systems all have significant differences from one another, exposing these differences could certainly help us understand the disparities and similarities in the perception of the right to silence in these three legal systems. However, in view of the breadth of the reflections that the development of the question would give rise to, as well as the limited framework in which we have had to place our study, we will limit ourselves to comparing the particularities of the legal traditions of continental law and *Common Law* [respectively attributed to the Belgian legal system on the one hand and to the English and American legal systems on the other], to see how the right to silence flourishes according to whether it is part of one or the other tradition, and to propose a synthesis of the answer to our question that was prompted by our initial reflection.

Finally, we will address some current cases implementing the right to silence before concluding our dissertation. We would like to point out that the cases we found interesting were in Belgium and the United States.

4.1 Cross-sectional analysis of England, Belgium, United States

4.1.1 Tradition of continental Law vs Tradition of *Common Law*

While the Belgian legal system has its origins in Roman law, it has been singled out as having a civil law tradition[297]. This is also called Romano-Germanic law, Romano-civil law, or continental law[298], we will sole refer to it as continental law in the following sections.

English law, on the other hand, is at the origin of the *Common law*, as is American law, which is strongly inspired by this *Common law*[299]. This is not without consequence. Indeed, the legal culture of countries governed by continental law differs greatly from that which is observed in legal traditions ensuing from the *Common law*. By legal culture, we mean here "the modern version of a people's mentality"[300], "the intellectual space in which judges have been trained and in which they evolve"[301].

In continental law systems, the law is conceived as a logical, organized framework, where institution and order have a predominant weight[302]. Moreover, the legislation is the primary source of this law [303]. Codification is undoubtedly the most characteristic technique of the laws of the Romanist family. The code is not a simple collection of rules, but a legislative edifice that is intended to reflect a harmonious city. It is supposed to provide the citizen with a readable manual to which it is always possible to refer and the judge, a valuable tool for grasping, through the arrangement of the principles and the classification of the rules, the legislative intention. Moreover, in this tradition, only the law is law, of which the judges are merely the spokespersons"[304]. In comparison to the continental law system, in the common law system the law "is less a series of legislative provisions, of which it would be possible to identify the date of promulgation or the others ", but rather a practice which is inscribed and recorded in the collective memory[305]. In these legal systems derived from the common law, one can even go so far as to speak of a "lack of understanding of the mechanisms of written law"[306].

In this way, the *common law*, from which the Anglo-American legal traditions originate, presents itself as an instrument that is offered to "a considered private actor, even required by it, as autonomous"[307] and capable of choosing what suits it best, in particular because of the initiative and responsibility that characterize it[308]. In England and the United States, it is a free man who is judged by his peers, in a public trial where each of the parties to the trial debates on an equal footing[309]. In this respect, we shall not fail to mention a significant example of this autonomy: the *plea bargaining*[310]. Both in England and in the United States, the litigant has control over the opening and the unfolding of the trial[311].

In this mechanism, which is extremely popular in the judicial situation in common law countries, the litigant is asked the ultimate question: "guilty or not guilty?"[312] Whether it is the *right of silence* in English law or the "*fifth*" in American law, both are oblivious to this question, the answer to which alone will determine the very future of the trial[313]. A virulent process of negotiation between the prosecution and the defense will then begin, and after several debates, they will be able to conclude a "plea agreement" within the framework of this "*plea bargaining*" procedure[314].

In the continental tradition from which the Belgian law originates, the contrast is striking. The pre-constituted order based on submission or compliance, which was built around the Roman law tradition does not presuppose as much individual freedom to its litigants[315].

The "paternalistic"[316] conception of power places the subject of the law in a position such that if he is recognized as having responsibilities, these are "limited or even castrated"[317]. This way of conceiving the individual is reflected in "the multiplication of chicanery, harassment, and procedural precautions [...]. The official himself, prisoner of a rational legal universe, entangled in its norms, finds autonomy only by interpreting the rule"[318]. For a full comparison, let us consider the guilty plea (see above). Although this mechanism now exists in Belgian law, which itself originated in the culture of haggling or "bargain"[319] recognized as a version of "plea-bargaining" in the Anglo-American legal tradition, is not articulated according to the same design[320]. Its introduction into Belgian law has even "underlined the uneasiness that exists in the Latin culture of settling in the field of criminal action"[321].

4.1.2 What right to silence in the Anglo-American and continental legal systems?

First of all, a distinction must be made between the conception of the right to silence in the Anglo-American tradition and that established in Belgian law. In Anglo-American law, the right to silence is primarily recognized as the right to remain silent[322]. It is also the right of the accused not to be compelled to testify or to incriminate him-/herself[323]. In Belgian law, on the other hand, the right to silence is conceived more broadly and involves the right to organize one's defense freely[324]. In this way, the accused who, in his defense strategy, allows himself the freedom to relate facts that are far from the truth will not be sanctioned[325].

Let us now consider the context in which this right to silence and the prohibition against self-incrimination are situated, depending on whether it comes from the Anglo-American tradition or from the continental law wherefrom the Belgian law originates.

The American is seen as a "rational individual, holder of rights"[326]. He is responsible for his destiny and cannot hide behind inattention or inadvertence to avoid answering for his acts or words. This explains the sacred importance as well as the almost theatrical character by which the litigants are opposed to the *Miranda Warnings*. This warning, when pronounced, "creates a certain coercive context, a suspended moment where this highly ritualized discourse finds its place in the ordinary space of the city"[327]. By issuing this warning, the litigant is made aware of his constitutional right to silence as well as the consequences that its exercise could possibly entail. Practice shows that these Miranda rights are often repeated several times, so that this autonomous and responsible individual can take responsibility for his or her own destiny in an enlightened manner[328]. Likewise, at the hearing, this empowerment of the litigant as master of his/her fate is not extinguished. The latter, if he/she chooses to speak in his/her own case, "is considered a witness: he/she is heard under oath and will be cross-examined by the prosecution, under penalty of perjury, he/she is obliged to tell the truth"[329].

In England, things are not so different. Indeed, if the accused wishes to speak at the hearing, he/she will also do so by taking an oath and thereby exposing him-/herself to perjury, if he/she allows him-/herself to insert in his/her defense facts that do not correspond to the truth.

The contrast in the understanding of the "right to silence" in Belgian law is striking. On the one hand, with regards to the contextual understanding of the right to silence; although it is considered to be one of the bulwarks of the criminal defense in Belgian law, there is no famous admonition establishing the right to silence, nor even a constitutional consecration attesting its existence. However, it has a basis in Belgian national law in Article 47 bis of the Code of Criminal Investigation (see above). Nevertheless, the establishment of the right in this statute is so timid that its fundamental character could be forgotten. On the other hand, one of the major differences with the English and American criminal systems is that there is no obligation in Belgian law for the accused to speak under oath, should he/she decide to speak in his/her own case at the hearing[330].

From this point, we perceive the fundamental cleavage between the Belgian system of continental law and the Anglo-American systems. The Belgian litigant will be able to organize his/her defense freely and make "statements that he/she considers useful"[331]. He/she will not be sanctioned if he/she maintains in the trial facts that do not correspond to reality, i.e., if he/she lies. In this regard, let us use the question appropriately posed by *Damien Vandermeersch:*

"Is justice not more humane if it allowed the accused to come to the trial with "his truth" which does not necessarily correspond to "the truth"? Should every suspect not be given a space for restraint, privacy, non-disclosure and even denial? Denial sometimes appears to the "stuck" accused as the only way to survive in the face of the serious accusations made against them: it is often very difficult, if not impossible, for a person to say the unspeakable or to confess the unmentionable"[332].

In addition to the above-mentioned differences between the English, American and Belgian penal systems, we can also say that these differences are notably the reflection of:

- An obsession with morality and the search for the truth beyond all reasonable doubt in the Anglo-American system, as opposed to a preference for the search for the truth that respects the rights of the defense in Belgian criminal law[333].
- The "taste" for morality which the Anglo-American traditions are borrowed from, in such a way that "the judicial practice recognizes a reversal of protection towards the one who in the course of the procedure adopts an *unfair* behavior so that they must be punished at all costs"[334].
- Disparities in the way criminal proceedings operate between the adversarial system, on the one hand, of which the United States and England are part, and the inquisitorial system, on the other hand, which is largely dominated by the Belgian criminal justice system, even if it is generally described as a mixed system[335].
- A divergence in the very conception of rights, so that in England and in the United States, rights are "themselves borrowed from a commercial nature"[336]. From then on, the litigant becomes a calculating being, *a homo economicus* constantly evaluating whether it is appropriate for him/her to adopt this or that

behavior when confronted with the legal machine. Therefore, this question formulated by *Ioannis Papadopoulos*, is also ours: "is it by chance that the progression of the *Common Law* goes hand in hand with capitalism? Does it not objectively accompany an infinite extension of the commercial sphere, whereas continental law is more concerned with preserving a public sphere?[337]

4.1.3 The Summary: Can the silence of the accused motivate a decision of guilt in England, the United States and Belgium?

We note that in England, the principle is the refusal to rely exclusively on the silence of the accused to justify a decision of guilt against him/her. However, this response has been nuanced. The first nuance consists in the possibility for the judge to draw inferences from silence about facts not mentioned during the interrogation but mentioned at the hearing. The second nuance is that section 35 of the Criminal Justice Order Act allows inferences to be drawn from the silence of the accused if the latter maintains his silence without this being justified by "serious reasons".

The third nuance to be made concerns the legislative changes that have occurred in English law. These have contributed to fragilize this already very shaky right to silence. Indeed, this new warning to the public is intended to be an encouragement to break the silence and to speak in preference to the police. This encouragement empties the law of all substance.

In our opinion, the stance of the person who resorts to his/her right to silence in England is by no means comfortable since he/she could expose him-/herself to the anger of the judges and the jury who, if they consider that his/her silence is maintained without serious reasons, could draw unfavorable conclusions. The only guarantee left to the accused is that his/her exclusive silence can never be used to justify a decision of guilt against him/her.

The question that remains to be asked is what should be understood by the term "serious grounds". This seems lame to us since this provision[338] implies the danger that at any moment, "serious grounds", a concept marked by subjectivity and therefore by a certain legal uncertainty, will not be assessed in the same way by the judges called upon to render their decision, and to interpret the silence of the one who maintains it (cf. The notion of common sense in the case law of the European Court of Human Rights).

In American law, the principle remains that it is not possible to draw conclusions from the silence of the accused and to use this silence to justify a decision of guilt against him/her when he/she has recourse to the Fifth Amendment. However, while it is conceded that the accused in this position will still enjoy the protection of the Fifth Amendment, we believe that, as a matter of fact, he or she will certainly lose it. As we said earlier, in the United States, when the accused wants to speak in court, he does so by promising to tell "the truth and nothing but the truth". Therefore, what remains of the right to silence and the privilege against self-incrimination if the person called to defend his own case is placed under oath? We consider that the American defendant is at this moment placed in an uncomfortable dilemma: either he alters the truth by perjuring himself, or he makes revelations that compromise himself. The fact that, in principle, it is forbidden to have recourse to the silence of the accused, when he/she avails him-/herself of his/her constitutional right to silence, and to the prohibition of self-incrimination in order to motivate a decision of guilt against him/her, should not distract us from the problem of the constraint imposed by the oath on the accused, when he/she decides to speak in court.

The choice remains for him/her to give honest answers to the questions that will be put to him/her and to oppose his/her right to remain silent when these would require answers that would place him in an uncomfortable position. Nevertheless, it is not excluded that adopting this posture could leave the impression to the judge and the jury that he is certainly guilty.

As for Belgian law, since it answers this question by conforming to the Strasbourg case law, the analysis of the posture of the European Court of Human Rights has enabled us to identify not only the answer of principle that should be attributed to Belgian law, but also the nuances that should be added.

In Strasbourg, the European Court of Human Rights is clear on the response of principle which intends to refuse the exclusive recourse to the silence of the accused in order to establish his/her guilt. Nevertheless, it qualifies this same answer with a consequent precision: "Only when the evidence against the accused calls for an explanation which the accused should be able to give, can the absence of an explanation allow the conclusion [therefore, silence], by simple common-sense reasoning, that there is no possible explanation and that the accused is guilty. Therefore, remaining silent from the beginning to the end of the proceedings may, in certain circumstances, have certain consequences". Incidentally, if it is true that the imperative of the search for the truth should not lead to an obsession with the right to silence, the respect required by the principles of the presumption of innocence and the rights of the defense should not lead to undermining it either. However, this explanation from the Court seems lame to us, since this justification implies the danger that at any moment, "common sense", a notion marked by subjectivity and therefore by a certain legal insecurity, will not be given the same assessment depending on the judges called upon to render their decision, and to interpret the silence of the person who invokes it.

The Belgian analysis continues with the reflections of certain doctrine authors. If in Belgian law, certain authors did not fail to seduce us with the assertion that not only was there a right to silence and a right against self-incrimination directly derived from the international conventions ratified by Belgium, but this right was also a right to lie for the litigant who resorts to this defense strategy when pleading his case. However, if in Belgian law, the case law of one of the highest Courts in the country precludes resorting exclusively to the silence of the accused to motivate his decision of guilt, it is not certain that this lie (which the exercise of the right to silence and the prohibition against self-incrimination supposes) does not have as a consequence the pronouncement of a heavier sentence against the person who uses it. This is done as a "punishment" to the person who, using his right, has taken the liberty of making the task of the judge who is supposed to render his decision on the basis of his own conviction more difficult by the lies (or silences) that he/she has uttered in support of his/her defense.

These nuances observed in Belgian law are not the only elements that contribute to the precariousness of this right. This fragility of the fundamental right to remain silent and not to incriminate oneself is attributable to the profound timidity with which this right was imposed in the Belgian legal system. The foundation of this procedural guarantee, which is one of the bulwarks of the criminal defense, is to be attributed to a few lost sentences in the Belgian code of criminal investigation. This reality makes it difficult for the litigant to become aware of this procedural guarantee, as well as of the real consequences that its application can bring about. In this perspective, it was not surprising to note that it was under the impetus of the case law of the European Court of Human Rights that a law was adopted in Belgian law to guarantee the accused the right to be assisted by a lawyer during the first interrogations; the lawyer, the emblematic figure of the protector of the rights of the defense, of which the right to silence is a part.

These findings in Belgian law have been attributed to the civil law tradition and the Belgian criminal law model, of which we are the heirs.

Finally, our study shows that silence **alone** is not sufficient to justify a decision of guilt against an accused in England, Belgium, and the United States. However, what does this mean in practice? The cases of Mehdi Nemmouche and Michael Cohen are two criminal cases that will allow us to see how the issue of the right to silence has been addressed in recent cases. Finally, we will conclude this dissertation.

4.2 Topical cases

4.2.1 *Nemmouche case*, the Jewish Museum attack: the Belgian case.

On May 24, 2014, around 3:30 p.m., a gunman entered the Jewish Museum in Brussels and killed four people[339]. *Mehdi Nemmouche* was accused of being the author of this quadruple murder. He was facing life imprisonment. On May 30, 2014, six days after the killing, Mr. Nemmouche was arrested as he got off a bus in Marseille while in possession of the weapons used in the museum, a revolver, and a Kalashnikov assault rifle.[340]

The case of the attack on the Jewish Museum is of particular interest to us because it involves a person who used his right to silence throughout the trial. He broke his silence during his verdict with the words "life goes on behind bars"[341].

From a right that was supposed to give "full force to the presumption of innocence, this right was supposed to protect suspects from abuse, pressure or what the courts modestly call abusive coercion"[342]. In this case, we are witnessing a regular in the penitentiary system who "opposes a singularly active silence that disarms the inquisitorial mechanism based on the search for the truth. With him no cooperation is possible. A war of positions is waged with the weapons of law diverted from their purpose"[343].

During his trial, *Mehdi Nemmouche* said nothing except "DAS, DAS, DAS" as a synonym for the invocation of the right to remain silent, which he decided to exercise before the judge. However, the material evidence gathered against him in four years of investigation was considered "overwhelming"[344]. Mr. Nemmouche's silence has been interpreted as a "silence of cunning, of contempt, of silent rebellion"[345].

His silence had several effects: it allowed the defense lawyer to "free up a space for speech"[346] and to focus on demonstrating that the attack on the Jewish Museum in Brussels was the result of an internal settlement of accounts by Mossad (the Israeli secret service), and that attacking *Medhi Nemmouche* was synonymous with having the wrong target, the only target being the Jews themselves. The silence thus allowed for a political defense[347]. In addition to engaging in the argument that consisted of invoking a kind of "moral equivalence between judge and accused and thus exonerating the latter"[348], silence also allowed the prosecution to "fight against this fanciful thesis" articulated by the defense lawyer who was trying, as best he could, to move the entire debate away from the search for the truth[349].

It is interesting for us to underline that the fact, for *Mehdi Nemmouche*, to resort to the right to remain silent was not the main element that convinced the judge when he found him guilty of the charges against him. It was the "overwhelming" evidence[350] that helped prove his guilt. In such circumstances, one may wonder what the underlying motivation was for choosing to remain silent. According to magistrate Denis Salas, making this choice is similar to a strategy aimed at preventing a debate on strongly supported evidence (images, expert reports, testimonies, etc.), and thus preventing his position from being weakened[351].

What we learned from this case is that silence, even if it concealed a ruse, sterilized the debate, and revolted the jurors, was not the essential element that justified the pronouncement of Mr. *Nemmouche*'s guilt. However, we cannot be certain that this silence maintained by the accused was not taken into consideration by the judge when determining the sentence for the accused.

Moreover, this case shows us that there is sometimes more to the use of the right to silence than a defense strategy. Indeed, it can be the solution behind which the accused who knows he is guilty of the reproached facts takes refuge, in order not to lose "the esteem of the group to which he claims to belong"[352].

Thus, commented the magistrate and essayist, *Denis Salas*, "no member of his family took the stand to testify on his behalf. On the contrary, his grandmother firmly disavowed his act. The accused, having committed a crime against humanity, even if he is not qualified as such, has left the human family. Therein lie the meaning of the silent certainty with which he wraps himself. For his peers, this silence is not a shield, but a banner: he is and will remain the one who has known how to resist the justice of the infidels (miscreants)[353]. The silence maintained by the person accused by society can be explained by the desire not to stray into endless explanations that would convince the judge, since at that moment, the author of the criminal acts knows that he will be rewarded in the afterlife by radical Islamism[354].

Conclusion

What can we think of the assertion that a man who remains silent is necessarily part of a desire to conceal the truth, or even to stifle his potential guilt that only a maintained silence could succeed in concealing?

What about the attitude of drawing negative conclusions from a refusal to express oneself and interpreting the silence of a person implicated as an admission of guilt?

While the right to silence is undoubtedly a fundamental right, it is in many ways vulnerable. Therefore, it would be wrong to assert that no conclusion could ever be drawn from the silence of the accused, whether in Belgian, English, or American law. In response to our initial question, "Can the silence of the accused spur the decision of guilt in England, Belgium and the United States? We answered in the negative, this answer, as we have seen, has been considerably nuanced.

However, given the breadth and complexity of the subject, we are aware that we have not been able to address all aspects raised by our question.

At this point, the only certainty that remains is that in these three penal systems, silence alone can never lead to a decision of guilt against the person who invokes it. Nevertheless, it can contribute, in particular circumstances, to support the motivation of this guilt.

Now, if we accept that a right is a legally protected interest, this protection, in order to exist, must be effective and guaranteed in all circumstances, subject to proportionate and justified restrictions. It cannot simply be consecrated by texts because the guarantee of texts is not sufficient.

In the end, what is the future of this litigant, who is often too clinging to the existence of a right whose subtleties or purposes he does not always understand? This right, the exercise of which alone sometimes imposes on him a posture of great fragility.

Destabilized by the brutality of the criminal trial, should someone, like *Nemmouche* or *Cohen*, cherished the ownership of a right that he claimed with pride, not have used his right more cautiously before the veil was lifted on the inconveniences that a simple silence could have generated?

***

The final words give way to advice that our attentive readers cannot ignore.

If you get into trouble while touring in the United States, and you get the famous Miranda Warnings, remember this: don't you dare say a word! This advice applies especially to the hearing since everything you say will be under oath. From then on, to all sorts of questions that will be asked of you, you will be compelled to say nothing but "the truth, and only the truth".

If you happen to have to answer for your actions in England, be careful! The warning that establishes your right to silence will be said to you in terms that will encourage you to give up that right by talking more to the police.

Keep in mind that if you give in and talk, all the facts that you do not share during the police interrogation, but that you reveal at the hearing, will expose you to the possibility of seeing your silence on certain facts work against you at the hearing.

Finally, if you happen to be questioned by the Belgian authorities, your fundamental right to silence, although it is communicated to you timidly, will allow you at the hearing to organize your defense according to your convenience, even offering you the possibility of distancing yourself from the truth when you present your defense.

However, be careful! If you are ultimately found guilty, the lies you told will certainly be the cause of a heavier sentence being handed down to you.

In the end, wherever you are, in England, Belgium or the United States, "you are the master of the words you have not spoken; you are the slave of the words you let slip out"[359].

Bibliography

I. Legislation

International Legislation

- European Convention for the Protection of Human Rights and Fundamental Freedoms, signed in Rome on November 4, 1950, approved by the law of May 13, 1955.
- International Covenant on Civil and Political Rights, signed in New York on December 19, 1966, approved by the law of May 15, 1981.

Legislation of the European union

Secondary law

- Directive (EC) No. 2013/48/EU of the European Parliament and of the Council of October 22, 2013 on the right of access to a lawyer in criminal proceedings and in proceedings relating to the European arrest warrant, on the right to inform a third party immediately upon deprivation of liberty and on the right of persons deprived of their liberty to communicate with third parties and with the consular authorities, O.J.U.E., L.294/1, November 6, 2013.

Belgian Legislation

Norms with legislative value

- Code of Criminal Instruction; art. 47 bis, art. 216.
- Law of July 20, 1990, relating to preventive detention.
- Law of 12 March 1998 on the improvement of criminal procedure at the stage of information and investigation, M.B., April 2, 1998.
- Law of August 13, 2011, amending the Code of Criminal Investigation and the law of July 20, 1990, on preventive detention in order to confer rights, including the right to consult and to be assisted by a lawyer, to any person heard and to any person deprived of liberty.
- Law of February 5, 2016 amending criminal law and criminal procedure and making various provisions relating to justice, M.B., March 1, 2016.
- Law of November 21, 2016, on certain rights of persons subjected to interrogation, M.B., December 02, 2016.

PARLIAMENTARY WORKS

- Draft law amending the Law of July 20, 1990, on preventive detention and the Code of Criminal Procedure, in order to confer rights on any person being questioned and any person deprived of liberty, including the right to consult, and be assisted by a lawyer, *Doc. parl.*, Senate, 2010-2011, No. 5-663/1.
- Draft law amending article 47 bis of the Code of Criminal Proceeding, *Doc parl*, Senate, 2009-2010, n°4-1720/1.

FOREIGN LEGISLATION

ENGLISH

- Northern Ireland Emergency Provisions Act 1987, art. 15 § 1.
- Criminal Evidence Northern Ireland Order 1988
- Prevention of Terrorism Temporary Provisions Act 1989
- Criminal Justice and Public Order Act 1994

AMERICAN

- American Constitution (*Bill of rights, 1787*), 5th and 6th Amendments.

II. CASE LAWS

EUROPEAN CASE LAWS

- Eur. Court of Human Rights, *Dobbertin v. France* ruling of February 25, 1993.
- Eur. Court of Human Rights, *Funcke v. France* ruling of February 25, 1993, Series A n° 256-A.
- Eur. Court of Human Rights, *Yagaci and Sargin v. Turkey* ruling of 8 June 1995.
- Eur. Court of Human Rights, *Murray v. United Kingdom* ruling of February 8, 1996, Appl. No. 18731/91.
- Eur. Court of Human Rights, *Saunders v. United Kingdom* ruling of December 17, 1996.
- Eur. Court of Human Rights, *Zana v. Turkey* ruling of November 25, 1997.
- Eur. Court of Human Rights, *William and Karen Condron v. United Kingdom* ruling of May 2, 2000.
- Eur. Court of Human Rights, *Liam Averill v. United Kingdom* ruling of June 6, 2000.
- Eur. Court Human Rights, *Daktraas v. Lithuania* ruling of October 10, 2000.

- Eur. Court of Human Rights, *Heaney and Mc Guiness v. Ireland* ruling of December 21, 2000.
- Eur. Court of Human Rights, *Thomas Tefner v. Austria* ruling of March 20, 2001.
- Eur. Court of Human Rights, *J.B. v. Switzerland* ruling of May 3, 2001, Rec.2001-III; I.
- Eur. Court of Human Rights, *Keith Beckles v. United Kingdom* ruling of October 8, 2002.
- Eur. Court of Human Rights, *WEH v. Austria* ruling of April 8, 2004.
- Eur. Court of Human Rights, *Gerda Rieg v. Austria* ruling of March 24, 2005.
- Eur. Court of Human Rights, *Jalloh v. Germany* ruling of July 11, 2006
- Eur. Court of Human Rights, *Pandy v. Belgium* ruling of September 21, 2006, Rev. dr.pén. 2007, p. 356.
- Eur. Court of Human Rights, *O'Halloran and Francis v. United Kingdom* ruling of June 29, 2007, JCP 2008, I, 110, n° 6, obs. Sudre.
- Eur. Court of Human Rights, *Salduz v. Turkey* ruling of November 27, 2008, Application No. 36391/02
- Eur. Court of Human Rights, *Zaichenko v. Russia* ruling of February 18, 2010.
- Eur. Court of Human Rights, *Pavlenko v. Russia* ruling of April 1, 2010.
- Eur. Court HR, *Brusco v. France* ruling of October 14, 2010.
- Eur. Court of Human Rights, *Dvorski v. Croatia* ruling of October 20, 2015, no. 25703/11.

English case laws

- R v. Rhodes, [1899] 1 Q B. 77 (C.A.).
- R v. WhiteHead [1929] 1 KB 99
- R v. Waugh [1950] A.C 203 (P.C.)
- R v. Chandler [1976] I WLR 585
- R v. Brownond Routh [1983] Crim. L.R. 38.
- R v.Waugh [2018] NZDC 1237.
- British Supreme Court ruling Al-Khawaja and Tahery v. United Kingdom of January 20, 2009, applications no. 26766/05 and no. 22228/06.

American case laws

Supreme court

- United States Surpeme Court, Hale v. Henkel, 201 U.S. 43 (1906)

- United States Surpeme Court, Twining v. New Jersey, 211 U.S. 78, 108-110 (1908).
- United States Surpeme Court, Griffin v. California, 380 U.S. 609 (1965).
- United States Surpeme Court, Miranda v. Arizona, 384 U.S. 436 (1966).
- United States Surpeme Court, United States v Nobles, 422 U.S. 225,230 (1975).
- United States Surpeme Court, United States v. Wilson, 420 U.S. 332 (1975).
- United States Surpeme, Court, Doyle v. Ohio, 426 U.S. 610 (1976).
- United States Supreme Court, Carter v. Kentucky: 450 U.S. 288 (1981).
- United States Surpeme Court, Rock v. Arkansas, 483 U.S. 44 (1987)
- United Supreme Court, Counselman v. Hitchcock, 142 U.S. 547 (1892).

COURT OF APPEALS

- U S Court of Appeals, (Third Circuit), United States v. Apfelbaum, 445 U.S. 115

BELGIAN CASE LAW

COURT OF CASSATION

- Cass. July 10, 1916, Pas 1917, I, 195.
- Cass. June 23, 1941, Pas, 1941, p. 250.
- Cass. June 6, 1881, Pas. 1881, I, 304.
- Cass. February 27, 1985, J.T. 1956, p. 506.
- Cass. May 13, 1986, RG 9136
- Cass. March 11, 1992, Pas, 1992, I, 618.
- Cass. May 6, 1993, Pas, I, 452
- Cass. September 30, 1993, Pas. 1993, I, 775.
- Cass. January 4, 1994, Pas, 1994, I, p.6.
- Cass. November 4, 1994, Pas. 1994, I, p. 6.
- Cass. (united ch.) February 16, 1996, Pas. 1996, I, 212
- Cass. December 9, 1997, Pas, 1997, I, 1382
- Cass. (united ch.), September 16, 1998, J.L.M.B., 1998, 1340.
- Cass. April 21, 1998, Pas, 1998, I, p. 464.
- Cass. January 13, 1999, Rev. Dr. Pén. 1999.
- Cass. July 20, 1999, Pas, 1999, I, p. 1044.
- Cass. April 5, 2000, Pas, I, p. 228.

- Cass. October 5, 2000, R.G. n° P. 10.0703. N.
- Cass. (2nd ch.) 10 December 2002, P. 02.1146.N.
- Cass. September 17, 2003, J.T. 2003, p.730.
- Cass. June 16, 2004, RG P040671.F.
- Cass. June 29, 2005, J.L.M.B., 2006, p.69.
- Cass (1st ch.), October 1, 2009, n° D.07.0024.N

COURT OF CONSTITUTION

- C.C., March 13, 2008, no. 50/2008
- C.C., September 22, 2016 no. 168/2016
- C.C., June 15, 2017, no. 76/2017

COURT OF APPEAL

- C.A., January 25, 2001, No. 4/2001

III. DOCTRINE

- AYAT, M., "Silence takes the floor: the breakthrough of the right to remain silent in comparative criminal law and in international criminal law", *archives de politique criminelle 2002/1 n° 24*, pp. 251-278.
- BENTHAM, J., *Traité des preuves judiciaires,* t. II, Paris, Bossanges, 1823, p. 451.
- BERTHE, E., and NEVE M., "A lawyer from the moment of arrest, a fundamental guarantee - The commitments to which Belgium has already subscribed and a glance at some of our neighbors", *J.T.*, 2010, pp. 726-727.
- BOSLY, H.-D., and VANDERMEERSCH, D., and BEERNAERT, M.-A., *Droit de la procédure pénale,* 6th ed., Bruxelles, La Charte, 2010, p.28.
- BOSLY, H.-D., and VANDERMEERSCH, D., and BEERNAERT, M.-A., *Droit de la procédure pénale,* 8th ed., Bruxelles, la Charte, 2017, p.26
- BOSLY, H.-D., and HENRI, D., "The conflict between the obligation to report and the accused's right to silence", *Rép. Not.,* Tome XVII, le droit pénal, Livre 1, Bruxelles, Larcier, 2014, n° 791.
- BOULOC, B., DE BECO R., LEGROS P., *Le droit au silence et la détention provisoire,*
- Buxelles, Bruylant, 1997, p.13.
- BOURSIER, M.-E., *Le principe de loyauté en droit processuel,* Paris, Dalloz, 2003, p. 153, n° 258.

- BULLIER, A.-J., and PANSIER, F.-J., *De la religion de l'aveu au droit au silence ou faut-il introduire en France le droit au silence des pays de Common Law*, Gazette du Palais, 8 February 1997, p.208.
- BULLIER, A.-J., "Plead guilty or not guilty" in *Réflexions sur le procès de common law,* Bruxelles, Bruylant, 2015, pp. 67 et 68.
- CARBONNIER, J., *Le silence et la gloire. D.* 1951. Chron. p. 119.
- CARTUYVELS, Y., CARTUYVELS, Y., "Police and prosecution in Belgium / towards a reconfiguration of powers?", *Droit et société* 2004/3 (n° 58), p.524.
- CHALUS, D., "The blind dialectic right to silence in the manifestation of judicial truth in comparative criminal law", *R.J.T., 2009*, p. 353.
- COPAIN, C., "The silence of the accused during the preparatory phase of the criminal trial in French law" *Cahier du droit,* Vol. 56, 2015, p.319.
- COSTE, J.-L., "Statute of speech and presumption of innocence", *AJ pénal*, Dalloz, 2004. p. 402.
- CUYKENS, S., HOLZAPFEL, D., and KENNES, L., "III.1. Can the silence of the accused justify the decision of guilt? » in *La preuve en matière pénale*, Bruxelles, Editions Larciers, 2015, p.81-115.
- DAURY-FAUVEAU, M., Orality in French criminal procedure (the right to silence), in *les procédures pénales accusatoires,* CEPRISCA Collection Colloques, 2012, p.13.
- DECLERCQ, R., *Beginselen van Strafrechtspleging*, 4th ed., Malines, Kluwer, 2007, n° 1685.
- DECLERCQ, R., *La preuve en matière pénale*, Prolégoména, vol. 13, Bruxelles, Swinnen 1988, 35.
- DEHERT, P., "The right to silence suspects and witnesses", *Vigiles*, 1999, n° 2, p.20.
- DINOUART, J., *L'art de se taire, principalement en matière de religion*, petite bibliothèque Payo, n° 794, 2011.
- DE LA SERNA, I., "The right to silence", *pli judiciaire,* 2015/32, p. 3-10.
- DELMAS-MARTY, M., "Criminal matters within the meaning of the European Convention on Human Rights, vagueness of criminal law", *Revue de science criminelle et de droit pénal comparé*, 1987, p.819.
- DE NAUW, A., *Initiation au droit pénal spécial*, Bruxelles, Story-Scientia, 1987, n° 122.
- DENNIS, I., « The Criminal Justice and Public Order Act 1994: The Evidence Provisions », [1995] *Crim.L.R.* 4, p.10.
- DE VALKENEER, C., *La tromperie dans l'administration de la preuve pénale : analyse en droit belge et international complété par*

des éléments de droit français et néerlandais, Larcier, janvier 2000, p. 487.

- ESSAID, M., *La présomption d'innocence,* La parole, Rabat, 1971, pp, 88 ets.
- FRANCHIMONT, M., JACOBS A., and MASSET A., *Manuel de procédure pénale*, Bruxelles, Larcier, 2012, p.1603.
- FRYDMAN, B., « Guilty or not guilty? », 23 mai 2011, disponible sur www.justice-en- ligne.be.
- GANSHOF VAN DER MEERSCH W.J., "The right of defense, general principle of law", in *Mélanges en l'honneur de Jean Dabin,* t. II, Bruxelles, Bruylant, 1963, p.594.
- GARAPON, A., ET PAPADOPOULOS I., *Juger en Amérique et en France,* ed. Odile Jacob, Paris, 2003, pp.47 and 49.
- GILMORE, G., *Ages of American Law*, New Haven (Connecticut), Yale University Press, 1977, p. 10.
- GIRARD, C., *Culpabilité et silence en droit comparé*, L'Harmattan, 1997, p.145.
- GREENHOUSE, C.J., "Anthropological Perspectives on the Americanization of Law",
- *Archives de philosophie du droit*, Paris, Dalloz, 2001, 45, p. 50.
- HOWARD, M. N., *Phipson on Evidence*, 15th ed., Londres, Sweet & Maxwell, 2000, p. 780.
- INCHAUPSÉ, D., The Anglo-Saxon criminal trial in *L'innocence judiciaire, Presses Universitaires de France,* 2012, pp.321-359.
- JACKSON, J., The *Right* of *Silence*: *Judicial Responses* to *Parliamentary Encroachment, Mod. L. Rev. Vol. 57, 1994, pp.595-596.*
- KENNES, L., *Manuel de la preuve en matière pénale*, Kluwer, 2009, pp. 111-117.
- KLEES, O., "From the obligation to testify to the right to silence", *Rev. Trim. D.H.,* 1994, 248-263.
- KONING, F., "I will only speak in the presence of my lawyer or the extension of the right to legal assistance at police hearings ('Salduz bis' law of November 21, 2016)", *J.L.M.B,* 2017, pp. 1092 to 1103.
- KUTTY, F., *Justice pénale et procès équitable,* t.II, Bruxelles, Larcier, 2006, pp. 205-328.
- LANGER, M., "The scope of accusatory and inquisitorial categories", *Revue de science criminelle et de droit pénal comparé, 2014/N° 4*, Dalloz, p.707-708.
- LEBOEUF, S., The role of the silence of the accused in comparative law, Thesis presented to the Faculty of Graduate Studies of Laval University as part of the doctoral program in law to obtain the PhD

degree in Law, Faculty of Law Université de Laval Québec, 2010, pp 34 and s.

- LEVY, L.W, *Origins of the Bill of Rights*, New Haven, Yale University Press, 1999, pp. 192-193.
- LIÉGEOIS, Y., « De "Sladuz+" wet van 21 november 2016: een nieuw hoogtepunt in het recht van toegang tot een advocaat onder dictaat van Europa », *Nullum Crimen*, 2017, p. 105.
- LIENG, R., The Royal Commission on Criminal Justice, The right of silence in police interrogation: A strudy of some the issues underlying the debate, Research Study No. London, 1993.
- MERLE, R., ET VITU, A., *Traité de droit criminel,* 5e éd., Cujas, 2001, t. II, n° 947
- MIRFLELD, P., «Two Side-Effects of Sections 34 to 37 of the Criminal Justice and Public Order Act 1994 », *Crim.L.R*, August 1995, p. 913.
- MOUFFE, B., "chapter 7 - procedural lies" in *Le droit au mensonge,* Bruxelles, Larcier, 2017, p.391.
- NICANG, B., "What is plea bargaining?", *Les Cahiers de la Justice.* 2012/3 N° 3, p19.
- OSIEL, M., *Juger les crimes de masse, La mémoire collective et le droit,* Seuil, 2006, p. 396.
- PETTITI, L.-E., *Droit au silence*. Documentação e Direito Comparado, n° 75/76, 1998, p105.
- PRADEL, J., *Droit pénal comparé,* 2e éd., Paris, Dalloz, 2002, p. 501 et 502.
- PROTAT, D., "The secular aspects in civil and criminal proceedings", *Revue internationale de droit compare*, Vol. 66 N° 3,2014, p.740.
- QUARRÉ, PH., « Le droit au silence », *J.T.,* 1974, pp. 525-528.
- RICHARD, J., *Psychiatrie gériatrique : esquisse d'une histoire médicale par l'élaboration de son langage*, Psychologie et sciences humaines, p.23.
- RICHARDSON, J., *Archbold: Criminal Pleading, Evidence & Practice*, Londres, Sweet & Maxwell, 2009.
- ROETS, D., "The right not to contribute to one's own incrimination in the case law of the European Court of Human Rights", *AJ pénal Dalloz Revue*, 2008, p. 119.
- SALAS, D., "the Jihad of silence. Observations on the trial of the attack on the Jewish Museum in Brussels (January 10 - March 18, 2019)", *archives de politiques criminelles*, pp.224- 230.
- SCHWARTZ, B., *The Bill of Rights: A Document History*, vol. 1, New York, Chelsea House Publishers,1971.

- STUART, L., « Miranda: The Story of America's Right to Remain Silent » *University of Arizona Press*, 2004, pp. 3-26.
- T. WAN, « The unnecessary evil of plea bargaining: an unconstitutional conditions problem and a not-so-least restrictive alternative », *Review of Law and Social Justice*, 2007, n° 17/1, p. 36.
- VANDERMEERSCH, D., "Continental law vs Anglo-American law: what lessons on Belgian criminal procedure law?" *Rev. Dr. Pén.*, 2001/16, p.515.
- VAN MEERBEECK, J., "The right to legal assistance in the light of the Salduz case law: the judicial power between Charybdis and Scylla", *J.T.*, 2010, n° 6398, pp. 381 à 388.
- VASSART, P., "The legs of Iseult or the paradox of the lawyer", in *Mélanges offerts à Raymond Vander Elst,* t. II, 1986, p.846.
- VOLO, P., *Le silencieux droit au silence*, Petites Affiches, 19 juillet 1934, p. 17.
- WAETERINCKX, P., « De (afgeleide) rechten van verdediging van de rechtspersoon. Heeft een rechtspersoon het recht te zwijgen, eventueel met of zonder bijstand van een raadsman? », *N.C.*, 2015, n° 2, p. 88.
- WAGNER, WJ., *« La preuve dans le droit des États-Unis », Recueils de la Société Jean Bodin pour l'histoire comparative des institutions,* Bruxelles, Librairie encyclopédique, 1963, p.417.
- WATTIER, I., "The right to remain silent, the right not to contribute to one's own incrimination and the right to assistance from one's lawyer", *Rev. dr. pén.*, 1996, pp. 960-967.

OTHERS

- Le Petit Robert de la langue française, 2011 Edition.
- Guide to Article 6 of the European Convention on Human Rights - Right to a fair trial (criminal section), 2014, p. 25.

IV. WEBOGRAPHY

- https://information.tv5monde.com/info/musee-juif-de-bruxelles-le-dossier-de-mehdi- nemmouche-vole-chez-un-avocat-282665
- https://www.nouvelobs.com/monde/l-amerique-selon-trump/20180426.OBS5736/michael-cohen-l-avocat-de-trump-invoque-le-droit-au- silence.html
- https://www.lejdd.fr/International/comment-donald-trump-sest-empetre-dans-laffaire- stormy-daniels-3643553
- www.justice-en-ligne.be
- http://loiseaumoqueur.com/?p=2403
- https://www.lexisnexis.com/uk/lexispsl/corporatecrime/document/391421/

591N-VY01- F188-N0SR-00000-00/Inferences_from_silence_overview

- (https://www.franceculture.fr/emissions/matieres-a-penser/le-silence-condition-ou- corruption-de-la-parole-publique-45-le-droit-au-silence-0)
- http://www.huyette.net/2017/06/le-droit-de-se-taire-et-le-droit-de-mentir-3.html
- https://books.openedition.org/puam/1474?lang=fr
- https://quizlet.com/87162947/partie-2-traditions-formatrices-du-droit-continental-et- principales-sources-au-2e-millenaire-flash-cards/

V. Filmography

- **Law & Order Special Victim Unit [New York Unité Spéciale]** (1999-present) by Dick Wolf.
- Episode 13 "Silence is Golden": ***How to get away with murder*** (2014-2020) de Peter Nolwak.
- **Miss Sloane** (2017) by John Madden.
- Remark by Ioannis Papadopoulos professor of law at the University of Thessaloniki - **Food for thought [series: speech, condition or corruption of public speech**, episode 4: The right to silence] (2020).

Endnotes

[1] Available at: http://hdl.handle.net/2078.1/thesis:26462

[2] J. DINOUART, *The art of being silent: mainly in matters of religion*, Payot, n ° 794, 2011.

[3] J. BENTHAM, *Treatise on judicial evidence*, t. II, Paris, Bossanges, 1823, p. 451.

[4] *Ibid.*

[5] Convention for the Protection of Human Rights and Fundamental Freedoms, signed in Rome on November 4, 1950, approved by the law of May 13, 1955, art. 10, M.B., August 19, 1955

[6] J. CARBONNIER, *Silence and Glory*. D. 1951. Chron. P. 119.

[7] L. -E. PETTITI, *Right to silence*, Documentatco e Diretio Comparado, n ° 75/76, 1998, p. 105.

[8] A.-J. BULLIER and F.-J. PANSIER, *From the religion of confession to the right to silence or should the right to silence in common law countries be introduced in France*, Gazette du Palais, February 8, 1997, p.208.

[9] C. COPAIN, "The silence of the accused during the preparatory phase of the criminal trial in French law", *Les Cahiers du droit*, Vol.56, 2015, p.319.

[10] B. BOULOC, R. DE BECO, P. LEGROS, The right to silence and provisional detention, Brussels, Bruylant, 1997, p.13

[11] The person targeted by criminal proceedings will successively be confronted with various authorities, each with distinct powers. This term is a generic term encompassing all these authorities required to carry out concrete actions in the context of a criminal prosecution.

[12] Eur Court. H.R., Funke v. France of February 25, 1993, Public. Eur. Court. H.R., Series A, No. 256-A; Court eur. D.H., J.B. v. Switzerland of May 3, 2001, Rec. 2001-III; I. DE LA SERNA, "the right to silence", judicial fold, 2015/32, p. 3-10.

[13] *Ibid.*

[14] I. DE LA SERNA, "the right to silence", judicial fold, 2015/32, p. 3.

[15] Definition of silence in Le Petit Robert de la langue française, Ed. 2011.

[16] I. DE LA SERNA, "the right to silence", op.cit., P.3.

[17] M.-E. BOURSIER, *The principle of loyalty in procedural law*, Paris, Dalloz, 2003, p. 153, No. 258.

[18] D. ROETS, "The right not to contribute to one's own incrimination in the case law of the European Court of Human Rights", Criminal Law, 2008, p. 119

[19] H.-D BOSLY, D. VANDERMEERSCH and M.-A. BEERNAERT, Law of criminal procedure 6th ed., Bruges, The Charter, 2010, p.28.

[20] International Covenant on Civil and Political Rights, done in New York on December 19, 1966, approved by the law of May 15, 1981, art. 14, M.B., July 6, 1983.

[21] D. VANDERMEERSCH, *Elements of penal law and criminal procedure, 5th ed.*, Brussels, the Charter, 2015, p. 765. [22] C.A., January 25, 2001, No. 4/2001; C.C., March 13, 2008, No. 50/2008; C.C., September 22, 2016, No. 168/2006; C.C., June 15, 2017, n ° 76/2017; Cass. (1st ch.), October 1, 2009, n ° D.07.0024.N; Cass. (2nd ch.), December 10, 2002, P. 02.1146.N.

[23] P. VOLO, *The silent right to silence, Petites Affiches*, July 19, 1934, p. 17.

[24] L. March 12, 1998 on the improvement of criminal procedure at the information and investigation stage, M.B., April 2, 1998.

[25] D. CHALUS, "The blind dialectic to silence in the manifestation of judicial truth in comparative criminal law", R.J.T., 2009, p. 353.

[26] *Ibid. ; J. PRADEL, Comparative Criminal Law, 2nd ed., Paris, Dalloz, 2002, pp. 501 and 502.*

[27] M.DELMAS-MARTY, "Criminal matters within the scope of the European Convention on Human Rights, vagueness of criminal law", *Revue de science criminelle et de droit penal comparé*, 1987, p.819.

[28] Court. H.R., Saunders v. The United Kingdom, December 17, 1996, §74. .

[29] Eur Court. H.R., Saunders v. United Kingdom, December 17, 1996, §74: "the public interest cannot justify the use of coerced answers in a non-judicial investigation to incriminate the accused in the criminal proceedings"; H. BOSLY, D. HENRI., "The conflict between the obligation to report and the accused's right to silence", Rep. Not., Volume XVII, criminal law, Book 1, Brussels, Larcier, 2014, n ° 791.

[30] Guide to Article 6 of the European Convention on Human Rights - Right to a fair trial (criminal aspect), 2014, p. 25, available at www.echr.coe.int

[31] "*The duty to testify in criminal proceedings is a good example of the normal civil obligations in a democratic society*"(Comm. C.E.D.H., decision B.B.C. v United Kingdom of January 18, 1996, D.R., 84, 129).

[32] *Ibid.*

33 R. DECLERCQ “proof in penal matters”, Prolégoména, vol. 13, Brussels, Swinnen 1988, p.35.

34 *Ibid.*

35 Cass., June 6, 1881, Pas., 1881, I, 304.

36 *Ibid.*

37 *Ibid.*

38 *Ibid.*

39 Cass., January 13, 1999, *Rev. Dr. Pen.*, 1999.

40 *Ibid.*

41 *Ibid.*

42 *Ibid.*

43 *Ibid.*

44 *Ibid.*

45 *Ibid.*

46 D. CHALUS, op.cit., R.J.T., 2009, p. 356.

47 Art 47 bis of the Belgian Code of Criminal Procedure; F. KONING, "I will only speak in the presence of my lawyer or the extension of the right to lawyer assistance during police hearings (‘ Salduz bis ’law of 21 November 2016)", J.L.M.B, 2017, pp. 1092 to 1103.

48 Eur. Court. H.R., Jalloh v. Germany ruling of July 11, 2006, §§ 113 and 114.

49 *Ibid.*

50 *Ibid.*

51 Eur Court. H.R., Heaney and Mc Guiness v. Ireland ruling of December 21, 2000, § 40.

52 O. KLEES "From the obligation to testify to the right to silence" Rev. Trim. D.H., 1994, 248-263, spec. 262; A. DE NAUW, Introduction to special criminal law, Brussels, Story-Scientia, 1987, n ° 122.

53 Cass. (united ch.), February 16, 1996, ruling known as Inusop, Pas., 1996, I, 212; Cass., March 11, 1992, Pas., 1992, I, 618.

54 Cass. (reunited ch.), September 16, 1998, ruling known as Agusta-Dassault, J.L.M.B., 1998, 1340.

55 In this regard, it should be recalled that the case law of the European Court of Human Rights attributes to the term "Accused" an autonomous meaning that goes well beyond the technical concept which prevails in Belgian law,

targeting the accused referred to the Assize Court to be tried there. According to this case law, the concept refers to any person charged with having committed a punishable act, but also to any person who has not been charged, but who is suspected of having committed an offense and who is therefore required to take measures to ensure its defense; H. D. BOSLY, D. VANDERMEERSCH and M.-A. BEERNAERT, Law of Criminal Procedure, op. cit., p. 30; M. FRANCHIMONT, A. JACOBS et A. MASSET, *Manuel de procédure pénale*, *op. cit.*, pp. 1246-1251.

56 Convention for the Protection of Human Rights and Fundamental Freedoms, signed in Rome on November 4, 1950, approved by the law of May 13, 1955, article 6, M.B., August 19, 1955.

57 International Covenant on Civil and Political Rights, done in New York on December 19, 1966, approved by law of May 15, 1981, art. 2, M.B., July 6, 1983..

58 J.-L. COSTE, "Statute of speech and presumption of innocence", AJ pénal, 2004. p. 402

59 Cass., June 29, 2005, J.L.M.B., 2006, p.69; Cass., September 17, 2003, J.T., 2003, p.730.

60 Eur. Court. H.R., Pandy v. Belgium of September 21, 2006, Rev. dr. pen., 2007, p. 356.

61 Eur Court. H.R., Daktraas v. Lithuania of October 10, 2000.

62 Cass., July 20, 1999, Pas., 1999, I, p. 1044.

63 F. KUTTY, *Criminal justice and fair trial*, t.II, Bruxelles, Larcier, 2006, pp. 205-328.

64 Cass., April 21, 1998, Pas., 1998, I, p. 464; Cass., January 4, 1994, Pas., 1994, I, p.6; Cass., November 4, 1994, Pas., 1994, I, p.6; Cass., September 30, 1993, Pas., 1993, I, p.775.

65 H. D. BOSLY, D. VANDERMEERSCH AND M.-A. BEERNAERT, Law of Criminal Procedure, 8th ed., Brussels, la Charte, 2017, p.26; R. DECLERCQ, Beginselen van strafrechtspleging, 4th ed., Malines, Kluwer, 2007, n ° 1685; Eur. Court. H.R., Gerda Rieg v. Austria of March 24, 2005; Eur. Court. H.R., Weh v. Austria, April 8, 2004.

66 I. WATTIER, "The right to remain silent, the right not to contribute to one's own incrimination and the right to assistance by one's lawyer", *Rev. dr. pen.*, 1996, pp. 960-967.

67 PH. QUARRÉ, “The Right to Silence”, J.T., 1974, pp. 525-528; P.DE HERT, “The right to silence of the suspects and witnesses”, Vigiles, 1999, n ° 2, p.20; L. KENNES, Manual of Evidence in Criminal Matters, Kluwer, 2009, pp. 111-117.

[68] *Ibid.*

[69] R. MERLE and A. VITU, *Treaty of Criminal Law*, 5th ed., Cujas, 2001, t. II, No. 947; M. ESSAID, *The presumption of innocence*, Rabat, ed. La parole, 1971, pp, 88 ets.

[70] W.-J. GANSHOF VAN DER MEERSCH, "The right of defense, general principle of law", *in Mélanges in honor of Jean Dabin*, t. II, Brussels, Bruylant, 1963, p.594.

[71] M. AYAT, "Silence takes the floor: the breakthrough of the right to remain silent in comparative criminal law and international criminal law", archives de politique criminelle 2002/1 n ° 24, pp. 251-278.

[72] *Ibid.*

[73] *Ibid.*

[74] Cass., May 13, 1986, RG 9136; Cass., January 13, 1999, RG P 98.0412. F, Cass., June 16, 2004, RG P040671.F.

[75] Cass., February 27, 1985, *J.T.*, 1956, p 506.

[76] Ibid. ; B. Mouffe, "chapter 7 - the procedural lie" in Le droit au mensonge, Bruxelles, Larcier, 2017, p.391; A. Schopenhauer, *Le fondement de la morale*, chap.XVII, "The virtue of justice", 1840.

[77] P. Vassart, "The legs of Iseult or the paradox of the lawyer", in *Mélanges offered to Raymond Vander Elst*, t. II, 1986, p.846.

[78] C. GIRARD, *Guilt and Silence in Comparative Law*, L'Harmattan, 1997, p.145.

[79] http://www.huyette.net/2017/06/le-droit-de-se-taire-et-le-droit-de-mentir-3.html

[80] M. DAURY-FAUVEAU, Orality in French criminal proceedings (the right to silence), in *accusatory criminal proceedings*, Ceprisca Collection Colloques, 2012, p.13.

[81] Eur. Court. H.R., Salduz v. Turkey of 27 November 2008, Application n ° 36391/02.

[82] *Ibid*,§ 55 ; See also Eur. Court H.R., Pavlenko v. Russia of April 1, 2010, no.42371 / 02, § 101, 1; Eur. Court H.R., Dvorski v. Croatia of 20 October 2015, no 25703/11, § 77. https://www.echr.coe.int/Documents/Research_report_absence_advocate_FRA.PDF

[83] Proposal for a law amending article 47 bis of the Code of Criminal Procedure, *Doc. parl.*, Senate, 2009-2010, n ° 4- 1720/1.

[84] J. VAN MEERBEECK, "The right to legal assistance in the light of the Salduz case law: the judicial power between Charybdis and Scylla", *J.T.*, 2010, n ° 6398, p. 382 ; P. WAETERINCKX, "De (afgeleide) rechten van verdediging van de rechtspersoon. Heeft een rechtspersoon het recht te zwijgen, eventueel met of zonder bijstand van een raadsman? », N.C., 2015, n ° 2, p. 88.

[85] F. KONING, ""I will only speak in the presence of my lawyer" or the extension of the right to legal assistance at police hearings", J.L.M.B., 2017, n ° 23, p. 1092.

[86] J. VAN MEERBEECK, "The right to legal assistance in the light of the Salduz case law: the judicial power between Charybdis and Scylla", J.T., 2010, n ° 6398, p. 382.

[87] In force at the time: Code of Criminal Procedure (art. 47bis and 62) and the law of July 20, 1990, on preventive detention (hereinafter L.D.P.) (art 2bis, 15bis and 16).

[88] Law of 13 August 2011 amending the Code of Criminal Investigation and the law of 20 July 1990 on preventive detention

[89] Directive (EC) n ° 2013/48 / EU of the European Parliament and of the Council of 22 October 2013.

[90] L. 21 November 2016, relating to certain rights of persons under interrogation, M.B., 02 December 2016.

[91] Y. LIEGEOIS, « De "Sladuz+" wet van 21 november 2016 : een nieuw hoogtepunt in het recht van toegang tot een advocaat onder dictaat van Europa », *Nullum Crimen*, 2017, p. 105.

[92] Eur. Court H.R., Zaichenko v. Russia ruling of February 18, 2010.

[93] *Ibid.*

[94] *Ibid.* § 52.

[95] Eur. Court H.R., Brusco v. France ruling of October 14, 2010, § 54.

[96] With Belgium being our main focus.

[97] Eur. Court H.R., February 25, 1993, Fuke v. France. Application No. 10588/83. Available at https://hudoc.echr.coe.int/fre#{"itemid":["001-62366"]}

[98] The European Commission of Human Rights was an emanation of the Council of Europe and, along with the ECHR, was part of the judicial system established by the European Convention on Human Rights. It "filtered" requests coming from States, organizations, or individuals. Since the European Court of Human Rights was made permanent on November 1,

1998, the Commission has been abolished and any petitioner can directly appeal to the ECHR.

99 Eur. Court H.R., February 25, 1993, Fuke v. France. Application n ° 10588/83, §6.

100 *Ibid.*, §7

101 *Ibid.*, §§8-9

102 *Ibid.*, §11.

103 *Ibid.*, §13.

104 *Ibid.*, §34.

105 *Ibid.*

106 *Ibid.*, §42.

107 *Ibid.*, 42 al.2.

108 *Ibid.*, §43.

109 Art. 6 § 1: "Everyone has the right to a fair and public hearing, within a reasonable time, by an independent and impartial tribunal, established by law, which will decide, either on disputes over his/her civil rights and obligations, or on the merits of any criminal charge against him/her".

110 Article 65 -1 of the Customs Code stipulates the following: "Customs officers having at least the rank of inspector and those in charge of the duties of collector may require the communication of papers and documents of any kind, relating to operations of interest and their department (…) ".

111 Eur. Court H.R., Funke v. France ruling of February 25, 1993, Public. Eur. Court H.R., Serie A, n ° 256-A, recital 50.

112 *Ibid.*, §45.

113 Eur. Court H.R., Gr. Ch., February 8, 1996, John Murray v. United Kingdom, Rec. 1996-I. RSC 1997 p. 476. Available at https://hudoc.echr.coe.int/fre#{"itemid":["001-62539"]}

114 *Ibid.*, § 11; Prevention of Terrorism Temporary Provisions Act 1989.

115 Criminal Evidence Northern Ireland Order Act 1988.

116 Eur. Court H.R., Gr. Ch., February 8, 1996, John Murray v. United Kingdom, §§ 11 - 16.

117 Northern Ireland Emergency Provisions Act 1987, art. 15 § 1.

118 Eur. Court H.R., Gr. Ch., February 8, 1996, John Murray v. United Kingdom, §11-16.

119 *Ibid.*

[120] Relevant passages of the aforementioned act (see note 83) read as follows:
Article 6
Conclusions that can be drawn from the failure or refusal to explain one's presence in a given location

1. Paragraph 2 of this article shall apply in cases where, during proceedings against a person charged with an offence, it is shown that:
   a) that person was arrested by a police officer at or about the time when the offence to which that person was apprehended was allegedly committed, and
   b) the police officer reasonably believes that the person's presence at that place and time may be attributed to the fact that the person contributed to the commission of that offence; and
   c) the officer informs the person of his/her suspicions, and asks the person to explain his or her presence, and
   d) the person fails or refuses to provide an explanation.
2. In cases of the application of this subsection
   a) the court responsible for determining whether to commit the case for trial or whether there are serious charges against the accused, and
   b) l the court or jury responsible for determining whether the accused is guilty as charged, may
      i. Draw such inferences, as is legally admissible, from the failure or refusal by the accused;
      ii. Consider on the basis of such inferences that such omission or refusal corroborates, or amounts to corroboration of, any incriminating evidence upon which the accused's omission or refusal takes on significance.
3. Subsections (1) and (2) shall not apply if the police officer, in asking the accused to explain his/her presence as provided in subsection (1)(c), has not indicated in ordinary terms what the effect of this section would be if he/she failed or refused to provide an explanation.
4. This section does not preclude the drawing of inferences which, outside the cases provided for in this section, may be based on the failure or refusal by a person to explain his or her presence in a particular place. (...)"

[121] Eur. Court H.R., John Murray v. United Kingdom ruling of 8 February 1996, §22.

[122] *Ibid.*, §36

[123] *Ibid.*

[125] *Ibid.*,§ 51.

[126] *Ibid.*,§56.

[127] *Ibid.*, §58.

[128] Eur. Court H.R., Saunders v. United Kingdom ruling of 17 December 1996, Rec. 1996 - VI. RSC 1997 p. Koering-Joulin, p. 478. Available at https://hudoc.echr.coe.int/fre#{"fulltext":["saunders"],"documentcollectionid2":["GRANDCHAMBER","CHAMB ER"],"itemid":["001-62568"]}

[129] *Ibid.*,§§14-18.

[130] *Ibid.*

[131] *Ibid.*

[132] *Ibid.*

[133] *Ibid.*

[134] *Ibid.*, §§ 19-25.

[135] *Ibid.*

[137] *Ibid.*, §60.

[138] *Ibid.*, §65.

[139] *Ibid.*, §68.

[141] *Ibid.*

[142] *Ibid.*, §71.

[143] Eur. Court H.R., 25 February 1993, Fuke v. France. Application no. 10588/83, §71.

[144] Eur. Court H.R., J.B. v. Switzerland ruling of 3 May 2001, JCP 2001, I, 342, no. 13, obs. Sudre; Eur. Court H.R., O'Halloran, and Francis v. United Kingdom ruling of June 29, 2007, JCP 2008, I, 110, n° 6, obs. Sudre.

[145] S. CUYKENS ET D. HOLZAPFEL, L. KENNES, "III.1. Can the silence of the accused motivate the decision of guilt?" in The evidence in criminal matters (La preuve en matière pénale), Brussels, Editions Larciers, 2015, p.81-115.

[146] Eur. Court H.R., Murray v. United Kingdom ruling of 8 February 1996, § 51-53.

[147] Reference is also made to "plausible" reasoning. Our remarks also apply to this term.

[148] Eur. Court H.R., Murray v. United Kingdom ruling of 8 February 1996, §§ 51-53.

[149] J. RICHARD, *Geriatric Psychiatry: Outline of a Medical History through the Elaboration of its Language*, Psychology and Human Sciences, Mardaga, 2001, p.23.

150 Dissenting opinion of Judge Martens, with which Judge Kuris concurs.

151 Eur. Court H.R., Saunders v. United Kingdom ruling of 17 December 1996, §69.

152 Eur. Court H.R., William, and Karen Condron v. United Kingdom ruling of 2 May 2000.

153 *Ibid.,* §§9-10.

154 *Ibid.*

155 *Ibid.*

156 *Ibid.*

157 *Ibid.*

158 *Ibid.*

159 *Ibid.*, §§13-17.

160 *Ibid.*

161 No comment.

162 The Kingston Crown Court

163 Eur. Court H.R., William, and Karen Condron v. United Kingdom ruling of 2 May 2000, §§ 23-28.

164 In the John Murray ruling, the Court observed that an experienced judge was charged with judging the facts, and that he had to give reasons for his decision to draw conclusions and explain the weight he gave to them. The exercise of discretion in this regard was subject to appeal before the appellate courts. It was therefore even more imperative to ensure that the jury was properly informed as to how it was to deal with the issue of the petitioner's silence.

165 Eur. Court H.R., William, and Karen Condron v. United Kingdom ruling of 2 May 2000, §48.

166 *Ibid.*

167 Eur. Court H.R., Murray v. the United Kingdom ruling of 8 February 1996, § 61 para. 2.

168 Eur. Court H.R., William, and Karen Condron v. the United Kingdom ruling of 2 May 2000, § 53.

169 *Ibid.,* § 55; on this question, see the teachings of point (2.1.4.)

170 Eur. Court H.R., Murray v. United Kingdom ruling of 8 February 1996, § 127.

[171] Eur. Court H.R., William, and Karen Condron v. the United Kingdom ruling of 2 May 2000, §62.

[172] Eur. Court H.R. (Third Section), Liam Averill v. United Kingdom, 6 June 2000.

[173] *Ibid.,* §§ 8-13.

[174] *Ibid.,* §14.

[175] *Ibid.*, § 24.

[176] *Ibid.,* § 51

[177] *Ibid.*

[178] *Ibid.*, §29.

[179] *Ibid.*

[180] *Ibid*,§49.

[181] S. CUYKENS AND D.HOLZAPFEL, L. KENNES, "III.1. *The silence of the accused...", op.cit. p.102.*

[182] *Ibid.*

[183] *Ibid;* Eur. Court H.R., Salduz v. Turkey ruling of 27 November 2008; E. BERTHE and M. NEVE, "A lawyer from the moment of arrest, a fundamental guarantee - The commitments to which Belgium has already subscribed and a glance at some of our neighbors", J.T., 2010, pp. 726-727

[184] Eur. Court H.R. (3rd section), Thomas Telfner v. Austria ruling of 20 March 2001.

[185] *Ibid.,* §§7-11.

[186] *Ibid.*

[187] *Ibid.*

[188] *Ibid.*

[189] *Ibid.*

[190] *Ibid.*

[191] S. CUYKENS and D. HOLZAPFEL, L. KENNES, "III.1. The silence of the accused...", op.cit, p.104.

[192] Eur. Court H.R. (3rd section), Thomas Telfner v. Austria ruling of 20 March 2001, §15.

[193] Eur. Court H.R. (Third Section), Thomas Telfner v. Austria ruling of 20 March 2001, §§ 17-18.

194 *Ibid.*, §15.

195 C Eur. Court H.R., Keith Beckles v. United Kingdom ruling of 8 October 2002.

196 *Ibid,* §§7-21.

197 *Ibid.*

198 *Ibid.*

199 *Ibid., 24* (On this point, see further development on English law).

200 *Ibid.*, §64.

201 *Ibid.*, §65.

202 *Ibid.*, §64.

203 Case law and doctrinal references confirming or sharing the teachings made in this point: CUYKENS AND D. HOLZAPFEL, L. KENNES, "III.1. The silence of the accused ...?" op.cit. pp.110-115; Eur. Court H.R., Zana v. Turkey ruling of 25 November 1997, §79; Eur. Court H.R., Quinn v. Ireland ruling of 21 December 2000, Application no. 36887/97; Eur. Court H.R., Yagaci, and Sargin v. Turkey ruling of 8 June 1995, § 66; Eur. Court H.R., Dobbertin v. France ruling of 25 February 1993 rendered unanimously, §43; C. BECCARIA, Offenses and Penalties, coll. Champs Paris Flammaron, 1979, p.70 R. Declercq, "Le droit au silence", Belgian Report to the IXth Congress of the International Academy of Comparative Law, Brussels, 1974, 611-626, spec. 624; J. Messine, "Recent developments in case law on criminal evidence" Liber, Amicorum José Vanderveeren, Brussels, Bruylant, 1997, 75-101, spec. 81; F. SUDRE, "European Convention on Human Rights, the right to a fair trial", J.-Cl. Cl. Europe, Fasc 6526, n° 158.

204 CUYKENS AND D. HOLZAPFEL, L. KENNES, "III.1. The silence of the accused... ?" op.cit. p.110.

205 *Ibid.*

206 *Ibid.*

207 *Ibid.*

208 C Eur. Court H.R., Gr. ch., 8 February 1996, John Murray v. United Kingdom, §§51-57.

209 CUYKENS AND D. HOLZAPFEL, L. KENNES, "III.1. The silence of the accused ... ?" op.cit. p.87.

210 *Ibid.*

211 *Ibid.*

212 Art. 47 of the Code of Criminal Investigation cited above:

§ 1. Before proceeding to the hearing of a person to whom no offence is imputed, the person to be questioned shall be briefly informed of the facts about which he/she will be heard, and it shall be communicated to him/her:

1) that he/she **cannot be compelled to accuse him-/herself;**
2) that his/her **statements may be used as evidence in court**; (...) All these elements shall be accurately recorded in a report.

§ 2. Before a suspect is questioned, the person to be questioned shall be briefly informed of the facts about which he/she is to be heard, and it shall be communicated to him/her (...)

3) that **he/she cannot be compelled to accuse him-/herself;**
4) that his **statements may be used as evidence in court**;

213 M. Beys, "What rights vis-a-vis the police?", J.D.J., 2014/5, n° 335, pp.5-16.

214 S. LEBOEUF, The role of the silence of an accused person in comparative law, Thesis presented to the Faculty of Graduate Studies of Laval University as part of the Doctor of Laws program for the degree of Doctor of Laws, Faculty of Law Laval University Quebec, 2010, pp 34 et seq.

215 https://books.openedition.org/puam/1474?lang=fr

216 Commentary by Ioannis Papadopoulos, Professor of Law at the University of Thessaloniki- Subject matter [series: Speech condition or corruption of public stance, episode 4: the right to silence] Available at: https://www.franceculture.fr/emissions/matieres-a-penser/le-silence-condition-ou-corruption-de-la-parole- publique-45-le-droit-au-silence.

217 Court of Chancellery

218 Contempt of the Court

219 C. GIRARD, *Guilt and silence in comparative law*, op.cit. p. 106.

220 *Ibid.*

221 *Ibid.*

222 *Ibid.*p. 111.

223 P. MIRFLELD, « Two Side-Effects of Sections 34 to 37 of the Criminal Justice and Public Order Act 1994 », *Crim.L. R*, 1995, p. 913.

224 Rule derived from 3 sections, 76, 78 and 82 of the Police and Criminal Evidence Act 1984 (PACE)

225 Criminal Evidence Act 1898, art.35.

226 R v. Chandler [1976] I WLR 585; R v. Brownond Routh [1983].

227 R v. WhiteHead [1929] 1 KB 99.

228 From CHARLOTTE GIRARD (see note 61). You do not have to say anything unless you want to, but anything you do say may be used as evidence (see note 178 in the book).

229 *Ibid.* You do not have to talk. But it may harm your defense, should you fail to mention something during the interrogation, which you will rely on later in court. Anything you say can be used as evidence against you (see footnote 180 in the book).

230 C. GIRARD, *Guilt and silence in comparative law*, op.cit, p 111.

231 *Ibid.*

232 In English law, the term "inferences", also called "adverse inference", refers to the unfavorable conclusions that the court is allowed to draw from the silence of the defendant. Available at: https://www.lexisnexis.com/uk/lexispsl/corporatecrime/document/391421/591N-VY01-F188-N0SR-00000- 00/Inferences_from_silence_overview

233 Criminal Justice and Public Order Act, art.34.

234 M.N. HOWARD, *Phipson on Evidence*, 15e éd., Londres, Sweet & Maxwell, 2000, p. 780

235 J. RICHARDSON (Éd.), *Archbold : Criminal Pleading, Evidence & Practice*, London, Sweet & Maxwell, 2009.

236 Criminal Justice and Public Order Act, art.35. Effect of accused's silence at trial.

(1) At the trial of any person for an offense, subsections (2) and (3) below apply unless— (a)the accused's guilt is not in issue; or (b)it appears to the court that the physical or mental condition of the accused makes it undesirable for him to give evidence; but subsection (2) below does not apply if, at the conclusion of the evidence for the prosecution, his legal representative informs the court that the accused will give evidence or, where he is unrepresented, the court ascertains from him that he will give evidence.

(2) Where this subsection applies, the court shall, at the conclusion of the evidence for the prosecution, satisfy itself (in the case of proceedings on indictment [with a jury] , in the presence of the jury) that the accused is aware that the stage has been reached at which evidence can be given for the defense and that he can, if he wishes, give evidence and that, if he chooses not to give evidence, or having been sworn, **without good cause** refuses to answer any question, it will be permissible for the court or jury to draw such inferences as appear

proper from his failure to give evidence or his refusal, without good cause, to answer any question.

(3) Where this subsection applies, the court or jury, in determining whether the accused is guilty of the offense charged, may draw such inferences as appear proper from the failure of the accused to give evidence or his refusal, **without good cause**, to answer any question.

(4) This section does not render the accused compellable to give evidence on his own behalf, and he shall accordingly not be guilty of contempt of court by reason of a failure to do so.

(5) For the purposes of this section a person who, having been sworn, refuses to answer any question shall be taken to do so without good cause unless—
   (a) he is entitled to refuse to answer the question by virtue of any enactment, whenever passed or made, or on the ground of privilege; or
   (b) the court in the exercise of its general discretion excuses him from answering it.

237 Ibid.

238 R v. Waugh [2018] NZDC 1237.

239 R. c. Rhodes, [1899] 1 Q.B. 77 (C.A.).

240 J. JACKSON, « The Right of Silence*:* Judicial Responses to Parliamentary Encroachment »*, Mod. L. Rev.* Vol. 57, 1994, *pp.595-596.*

241 Translation from CHARLOTTE GIRARD's book (see note 61): A person shall not have the proceedings against him/her transferred to the Royal Court for trial, have to answer or be convicted for an offence solely on the grounds of an inference drawn from a failure or refusal as mentioned in Art. 34, subsection (2), Art. 35, subsection (2) or Art. 37, subsection (2); Criminal Justice and Public Order Act, Art. 38.

242 Eur. Court, H.R., William, and Karen Condron v. United Kingdom ruling of 2 May 2000, § 56.

243 Annuaire français de droit international, volume 11, 1965; https://home.kpmg/fr/fr/home/insights/2019/03/decryptages-une-singularite-americaine-le-grand-jury.html

244 Summary of the case obtained from http://loiseaumoqueur.com/?p=2403; L STUART, "*Miranda: The Story of America's Right to Remain Silent*", University of Arizona Press, 2004, pp. 3-26; United States Supreme Court, *Miranda v. Arizona*, 384 U.S. 436 (1966).

245 *Ibid.*

246 *Ibid*

247 *Ibid.*

248 *Ibid.*

249 *Ibid.*

250 *Ibid.*

251 *Ibid.*

252 The Sixth Amendment of the US Bill of Rights refers to the right to a fair trial. In all criminal proceedings, the accused shall have the right to a speedy and public trial by an impartial jury of the State and district in which the crime was committed - the district having been previously delimited by law - to be informed of the nature and cause of the charge, to be confronted with the witnesses against him, to require by lawful means the attendance of the defense witnesses, and to have the assistance of counsel for his defense. Translation from The wolrd book Encyclopedia - The Constitution of the United States of America. 2004 (Available at: https://fr.usembassy.gov/wp-content/uploads/sites/50/2017/06/pub_constitution.pdf)

253 Annuaire français de droit international, volume 11, 1965; https://home.kpmg/fr/fr/home/insights/2019/03/decryptages-une-singularite-americaine-le-grand-jury.html

253 Summary of the case partially obtained from http://loiseaumoqueur.com/?p=2403; L STUART, "*Miranda: The Story of America's Right to Remain Silent*", University of Arizona Press, 2004, pp. 3-26; United States Supreme Court, *Miranda v. Arizona*, 384 U.S. 436 (1966); https://www.oyez.org/cases/1965/759; *The American Civil Liberties Union, ACLU.*

254 "Sir, you have these rights under the Supreme Court's decision of *Miranda* v. *Arizona.* You have the right to remain silent and anything you say can and may be used against you; you have a right to have a lawyer present prior to and during any questioning; if you can't afford a lawyer and you want one, one will be appointed for you; and, you have a right to terminate this interview at any time".

255 Annuaire français de droit international, volume 11, 1965; https://home.kpmg/fr/fr/home/insights/2019/03/decryptages-une-singularite-americaine-le-grand-jury.html

256 Examples: Episode 13 "Silence is Golden": Peter Nolwak's How to Get Away with Murder (2014-2020); John Madden's Miss Sloane (2017); Dick Wolf's New York Special Unit (1999-present).

257 S. LEBOEUF, The role of the silence of the accused in comparative law, op.cit, pp 34 et seq.

258 L. LEVY, « Origins of the Bill of Rights », New Haven, Yale University Press, 1999, pp. 192-193.

259 I plead the Fifth Amendment

260 The entirety of the Fifth Amendment to the U.S. Constitution (The Bill of Rights 1789): *No person shall be held to answer for a capital or infamous crime unless indicted or tried by a grand jury, except in cases of acts committed in the land or naval forces, or in the militia, in active service in time of war, or public peril; no one may twice for the same offense be threatened in his life or in his person; no one may be compelled to testify against himself in a criminal trial, nor be deprived of his life, liberty or property without due legal procedure; no expropriation in the public interest will be possible without fair compensation*".

261 Comments by Ioannis Papadopoulos Professor of Law at the University of Thessaloniki – *Matières à penser* [series: The condition or corruption of public speech, episode 4: The right to silence].

262 B. SCHWARTZ, *The Bill of Rights: A Document History*, vol. 1, New York,Chelsea House Publishers,1971.

263 United States Supreme Court, Twining c. New Jersey, 211 U.S. 78, 108-110(1908).

264 United States Supreme Court, United States v Nobles, 422 U.S. 225 230 (1975).

265 United States Supreme Court, Twining c. New Jersey, 211 U.S. 78, 108-110(1908).

266 B. SCHWARTZ, *The Bill of Rights, op.cit.*, p. 65.

267 *Ibid.*

268 United States Supreme Court, *Rock v. Arkansas*, 483 U.S. 44 (1987); *« in fact, the most important witness for the defense in many criminal cases is the defendant himself. There is no justification today for a rule that denies an accused the opportunity to offer his own testimony. Like the truthfulness of other witnesses, the defendant's veracity, which was the concern behind the original common law rule, can be tested adequately by cross-examination* ».

269 Ibid.

270 United States Supreme Court, *Hale* v. *Henkel*, 201 U.S. 43 (1906); United States Supreme Court, U.S. Supreme Court. *Counselman* v. *Hitchcock*, 142 U.S. 547 (1892).

271 United States Court of Appeals, (Third circuit), United States v. Apfelbaum, 445 U.S.115.

272 United States Supreme, Court, Doyle v. Ohio, *426 U.S. 610* (*1976*).

273 United States Supreme Court, *United States* v. *Wilson*, 420 *U.S.* 332 (1975).

274 United States Supreme Court, *Griffin* v. *California*, 380 U.S. 609 (1965).

275 United States Supreme Court, Carter v. Kentucky : 450 U.S. 288 (1981).

276 S. LEBOEUF, The role of the silence of the accused in comparative law, op.cit. 2010, p. 303.

277 Ioannis Papadopoulos, Professor of Law at the University of Thessaloniki, in « *Matières à penser* » [series: the condition or corruption of public speech, episode 4: The right to silence].

278 *Ibid.*

279 "Do you swear to tell the truth, the whole truth and nothing but the truth?" is the phrase that individuals who swear an oath say in an American court of law: B. FRYDMAN, "Guilty or not guilty?", 23 May 2011, available at www.justice-en-ligne.be

280 P. QUARRE, "The right to silence," J.T., 1974, pp. 525.

281 Ibid.

282 C. DE VALKENEER, *Deception in the administration of criminal evidence: analysis in Belgian and international law supplemented by elements of French and Dutch law,* Larcier, janvier 2000, p. 487.

283 Cass., 23 juin 1941, *Pas*., 1941, p. 250.

284 M. PETITI, dissenting opinion under the Eur. Court H.R., Murray v. United Kingdom ruling of 8 February 1996, Reports, 1996- 1, pp. 62-63.

285 F. KUTY, obs. under Cass. 27 April 1997, J.L.M.B., 1998, p. 667, obs. pp. 668-670 "The general principle of the freedom to organize the defense and the motivation of sentences".

286 *Ibid.*

287 Cass., 10 July 1916, Pas 1917, I, 195.

288 Cass., 5 April 2000, Pas, I, p. 228.

289 *Ibid.*

290 *Ibid.*

291 Cass., 5 October 2000, R.G. n° P. 10.0703. N.

292 *Ibid.*

293 *Ibid.*

294 *Ibid.*

[295] To cite but a few examples: Cass, 13 January 1999, *Rev.dr.pén*, 1999,904; Cass (ch. Réun.), 16 February 1996, Pas, I, 212; Cass, 6 May 1993, Pas, I, 452; Cass, 9 December 1997, Pas, 1997, I, 1382.

[296] O. KLEES, From the right to silence to that of lying, December 3, 2017, available at https://www.justice-en- ligne.be/Du-droit-au-silence-a-celui-de: "This practice is full of examples demonstrating that, if the judge is convinced that certain defense arguments are only untruths, he will condemn more severely than in the opposite case."

[297] https://quizlet.com/87162947/partie-2-traditions-formatrices-du-droit-continental-et-principales-sources-au-2e- millenaire-flash-cards/

[298] *Ibid.*

[299] A. A. GARAPON AND I. PAPADOPOULOS, Judging in America, and France, éd. Odile Jacob, Paris, 2003, p.47 and 49: "Even if the United States was built partly on the foundation of a common law legal culture, it has made major modifications to it (...) However, these differences with the common law do not bring American legal culture closer to Europe, quite the contrary"; G. GILMORE, Ages of American Law, New Haven (Connecticut), Yale University Press, 1977, p. 10: "The genius of American law resides, according to some, in this constructive combination of the two great Western models of the civil law and the common law.

[300] A. GARAPON and I. PAPADOPOULOS, *Judging in America, and France*, op.cit, p.21.

[301] *Ibid.*, p.50.

[302] *Ibid.* [303] *Ibid.* [304] *Ibid.*, p.23.

[305] *Ibid.*, p.51

[306] D. INCHAUPSÉ, The Anglo-Saxon Criminal Trial in *L'innocence judiciaire, Presses Universitaires de France*, 2012, pp.321-359: "In the United States, where statutes passed in principle take precedence over classical Common Law, it often happens that certain texts punish an offence without giving it a definition. These so-called "reception statutes" merely incorporate into their positive law an offence that is supposed to already exist in the common law", explains Dominique Inchaupsé.

[307] GARAPON et I. PAPADOPOULOS, *Judging in America, and France*, *op.cit.*, p.65.

[308] *Ibid.*

[309] British Supreme Court ruling on *Al-Khawaja and Tahery v. United Kingdom* of January 20, 2009, applications no. 26766/05 and no. 22228/06.

310 B. NICANG, *"What is Plea Bargaining?"*, Les Cahiers de la Justice, 2012/3 No. 3, pp. 89-101: Plea bargaining or negotiated plea is an admission of guilt preceded by a bargaining on the sentence. It is a simplified trial procedure that avoids a trial on guilt through settlement. The plea bargain is an agreement between a prosecutor and a defendant in which the defendant waives the exercise of constitutional prerogatives and pleads guilty to a lesser offense or to one of several charges in exchange for some concessions from the prosecutor, which may include a recommendation for a lenient sentence and/or reduction of the charges regardless of the seriousness of the offense. In our country, the guilty plea and other alternative methods do not follow the same logic and are not part of an idea of greater autonomy, but of reducing the judicial backlog

311 *Ibid.*

312 A.-J. BULLIER, "Pleading guilty or not guilty" in Réflexions sur le procès de common law, Brussels, Bruylant, 2015, pp. 67 and 68.

313 *Ibid.*

314 B. FRYDMAN, "Guilty or not guilty?", op. cit; T. WAN, "The unnecessary evil of plea bargaining: an unconstitutional conditions problem and a not-so-least restrictive alternative", Review of Law and Social Justice, 2007, n° 17/1, p. 36.

315 A. GARAPON et I. PAPADOPOULOS, *Judging in America, and France, op.cit.*, p.65.

316 Ioannis Papadopoulos on France in "*Matières à penser*" [series: the condition or corruption of public speech, episode 4: The right to silence].

317 A. GARAPON et I. PAPADOPOULOS, *Judging in America, and France, op.cit.*, p.65.

318 *Ibid.*, p.66.

319 See (4.1.2). Latest developments on the "market character" of rights in countries with a Common Law legal tradition.

320 In Belgium, unlike in the USA and England, it is not systematically offered. In addition, a "guilty plea" can only be used for certain offences and under specific conditions. See. Law of 5 February 2016, amending criminal law and criminal procedure and stipulating various provisions relating to justice, M.B., February 19, 2016 (This law is also known as "potpourri II". In its articles 96 and 97 it inserts the new article 216 in the Code of Criminal Investigation, which entered into force on February 29, 2016. This provision provides that it will now be possible for any suspect or defendant to benefit from the new procedure known as "Prior Acknowledgement of Guilt". This allows the suspect/accused to benefit from a lighter sentence,

provided that he/she acknowledges his/her guilt. For this procedure to be applicable, it is necessary that the facts are not punishable, in concreto, by a principal correctional imprisonment of more than five years.

321 https://justice.belgium.be/fr/nouvelles/autres_communiques_63

322 D. VANDERMEERSCH, "Continental law vs Anglo-American law: what lessons are drawn from the Belgian Criminal Procedure Law?" Rev. Dr. Pén, 2001/16, p.515.

323 *Ibid.*

324 *Ibid.*

325 *Ibid.*

326 C. J. GREENHOUSE, "Anthropological Perspectives on the Americanization of Law", *Archives de philosophie du droit, Paris*, Dalloz, 2001, 45, p. 50.

327 Ioannis Papadopoulos on France in "Matières à penser" [series: the condition or corruption of public speech, episode 4: The right to silence].

328 Ioannis Papadopoulos professor of law at the University of Thessaloniki in "Matières à penser" [series: the condition or corruption of public speech, episode 4: The right to silence].

329 D. VANDERMEERSCH, "Continental law vs Anglo-American law...", op.cit, p.515.

330 O. KLEES, From the right to Silence to that of lying, *op.cit.* https://www.justice-en-ligne.be/Du-droit-au-silence-a- celui-de

331 D. VANDERMEERSCH, "Continental law vs Anglo-American law...", *op.cit.*, p.517.

332 Ibid.

333 Ibid.

334 D. INCHAUPSÉ, The Anglo-Saxon Criminal procedure in *L'innocence judiciaire, Presses Universitaires de France*, 2012, pp.321-359.

335 Y. Cartuyvels. Police and prosecution in Belgium / towards a reconfiguration of powers? Droit et société 2004/3 (n° 58), p.524

338 Criminal Justice and Public Order Act, art.35.

339 https://information.tv5monde.com/info/musee-juif-de-bruxelles-le-dossier-de-mehdi-nemmouche-vole-chez-un- avocat-282665

340 *Ibid.*

[341] D. SALAS, the Jihad of silence. Observations on the trial of the attack on the Jewish Museum in Brussels (10 January - 18 March 2019), Criminal Policy Archives, p.223.

[342] *Ibid.*

[343] *Ibid., p.224.*

[344] *Ibid.*

[345] *Ibid.*

[346] *Ibid.*

[347] *Ibid., p.227.*

[348] M. OSIEL, *Judging mass crimes, Collective memory, and law*, Seuil, 2006, p. 396.

[349] D. SALAS, the Jihad of Silence, op.cit, p.*227.*

[350] *See.* John Murray jurisprudence which refers to the notion of "overwhelming charges".

[351] The police and the investigating judges who testified openly in Belgium gathered no less than "twenty-three pieces of damning evidence". During the trial, two investigating judges, seated in the center of the courtroom, directed the proceedings for seven days, giving the floor to the twenty-seven investigators as they testified before the jurors.

[352] D. SALAS, the Jihad of silence, *op.cit., p.227.*

[353] *Ibid.,* p.229.

[354] *Ibid.,* p.230.

[355] Summary entirely borrowed from the following sites: https://www.lejdd.fr/International/comment-donald-trump-sest-empetre-dans-laffaire-stormy-daniels-3643553; https://www.nouvelobs.com/monde/l-amerique-selon-trump/20180426.OBS5736/michael-cohen-l-avocat-de-trump-invoque-le-droit-au-silence.html

[356] As well as Donald Trump himself. However, the proceeding was against Micahel Cohen.

[359] Lao-Tseu

Made in United States
Orlando, FL
04 November 2026

90206381R00056